THE MEANING OF MONEY IN CHINA AND THE UNITED STATES

T0351272

HAU
BOOKS

www.haubooks.com

THE MEANING OF MONEY IN CHINA AND THE UNITED STATES

THE 1986 LEWIS HENRY MORGAN LECTURES

Emily Martin

Foreword by Eleana J. Kim
Afterword by Jane I. Guyer and Sidney Mintz

Hau Books
Chicago

Published as part of the Hᴀᴜ-Morgan Lectures Initiative in collaboration with the Department of Anthropology at the University of Rochester.

Cover and layout design: Sheehan Moore
Typesetting: Prepress Plus (www.prepressplus.in)

ISBN: 978-0-9905050-2-0
LCCN: 2014953507

Hᴀᴜ Books
Chicago Distribution Center
11030 S. Langley
Chicago, IL 60628
www.haubooks.com

Hᴀᴜ Books is marketed and distributed by The University of Chicago Press.
www.press.uchicago.edu

Printed in the United States of America on acid-free paper.

Contents

Foreword

The Lewis Henry Morgan lectures at the University of Rochester were inaugurated in 1962 and have been presented annually ever since. The lectures commemorate not only Morgan's contributions to the founding of the University of Rochester and his support for the founding of a women's college, but also his legacy in anthropology, as reflected in the topics of the first three lectures, which focused on kinship (Meyer Fortes, 1963), native North Americans (Fred Eggan, 1964), and technology and social evolution (Robert M. Adams, 1965).

As the oldest and longest-running such lecture series in North America, the Morgan Lectures have produced some of the most influential texts in modern anthropology, to name but a few: Victor Turner's *The Ritual Process*, Marilyn Strathern's *After Nature*, and Nancy Munn's *The Fame of Gawa*. A view of the lectures after more than fifty years illustrates the ways that anthropologists have moved well beyond Morgan's Enlightenment roots, and also how they have expanded upon the topics that preoccupied him: kinship and social organization, political economy, indigenous peoples, and cross-cultural comparison.

Many of the lectures have culminated in the publication of an original monograph. Some of them that have not yet appeared in print will now enjoy a second life online and in new print editions, thanks to a new collaboration with HAU, which will bring past, unpublished lectures to a wider audience. In addition, more recent lectures will be available in streaming video format on HAU's website.

We are delighted to present Emily Martin's public lectures, *The meaning of money in China and the United States*, which were first delivered in 1986 and are presented here for the first time in their entirety. These four lectures combine ethnographic richness, conceptual brilliance, and cultural critique, connecting with Morgan's interest in property and his comparative approach. They offer an illuminating analysis of money, value, and morality through the lenses of rural Taiwanese social life and the pursuits of prosperity among a Methodist sect in urban Baltimore. With the passage of time, they have remained lucid and fascinating. Moreover, they have proven to be prescient, as debt, money, currency, and finance capital would become objects of renewed ethnographic attention especially at the turn of the millennium.

We extend heartfelt thanks to Emily for her graciousness and enthusiasm for this project. We also thank Giovanni da Col and Sean Dowdy for their energetic investment in this collaboration, and are grateful to their colleagues at Hau for their careful attention throughout the production process.

Eleana J. Kim
Rochester, April 2014

Acknowledgments

I would like to thank the faculty of the Department of Anthropology at the University of Rochester, who invited me to give these lectures in 1986. I am especially grateful to Anthony Carter, who was warmly encouraging and consistently helpful before, during, and after my visit. In 2014 Eleana Kim continued this tradition of care and attention, and I thank her. I am grateful to the editorial staff of Hau for making the preparation of the manuscript orderly and efficient. In particular, I thank Sheehan Moore for the cover design and editing of figures, Giovanni da Col and Robert Foster for organizing the publication and inaugurating the Hau-Morgan Lectures Initiative, and Jane Guyer and Sidney Mintz for their new afterword. Justin Dyer's conscientious and skillful editing was essential, and Sean Dowdy's organized management made the process flow smoothly. I thank my family—Richard, Jenny, and Ariel—for their patience during the preparation of these lectures in 1986 and in again in 2015.

EMILY MARTIN
New York City, February 2015

List of Figures

Figure 12. Nineteenth-century tea dealers.

Figure 13. Nineteenth-century individual cells for the governmental examinations.

Figure 14. Merchants wearing furs and silk.

Figure 15. Aerial view of terraced rice fields.

Figure 16. Nineteenth-century silk reelers.

Figure 17. Nineteenth-century embroiderers.

Figure 18. The five grains in a rice measure in Taiwan. Photo by the author.

Figure 19. The eldest son holding the rice measure in Taiwan. Photo by the author.

Figure 20. Kitchen god behind the stove in Fukien province. Photo by the author.

Figure 21. Close-up of image of kitchen god in Fukien province. Photo by the author.

Figure 22. New Year's house cleaning in Taiwan. Photo by the author.

Figure 23. Rice harvesting in Taiwan. Photo by the author.

Figure 24. Gifts being brought to the bride in Taiwan. Photo by the author.

Figure 25. Gifts to the bride in Taiwan. Photo by the author.

Figure 26. A bride with gifts arranged behind her in Taiwan. Photo by the author.

Introduction

WORKING UP TO THE 1986 MORGAN LECTURES

When I wrote the 1986 Morgan Lectures, I was working in the early days of the anthropology department at Johns Hopkins University. They were written as part and parcel of my own intellectual path, but that path was strongly influenced by the department's environment.

My immediate colleagues included Sidney Mintz, Katherine Verdery, Gillian Feeley-Harnik, Michel-Rolph Trouillot, Ashraf Ghani, Beatriz Lavandera, and Richard and Sally Price. So close that they might well have been in the department were David Harvey, Erica Schoenberger (geographers), and David Cohen (historian). Sidney Mintz set about leavening the mix by adding various luminaries for short visits or semester long residencies: Claude Lévi-Strauss, Raymond Firth, Edmund Leach, Maurice Bloch, Fredrik Barth, and Arturo Warman. Encountering and conversing with these scholars in the flesh was immensely rewarding, for they stayed with us long enough to burst the bounds of our rather parochial American obsessions. We learned the long story of their early, middle, and late research projects, their different academic homes, and the different ways they engaged with anthropological theory over the decades. We were confronted deeply with different national styles of anthropology, attached of course to different colonial histories: French anthropology, British anthropology from the London School of Economics to Cambridge University, Mexican anthropology, and Norwegian anthropology.

The most remarkable feature of that environment was its lack of dogma. At the beginning of the department's founding, we emerged as a group from a fractious atmosphere in anthropology. At the time the subtopics within the field were fairly well defined: economic anthropology, symbolic anthropology, linguistic anthropology, political anthropology, anthropology of religion, and so on. Students had to work within these boxes and faculty were expected to identify themselves in terms of them. At the time, anthropologists were exercised over who would win the battle between materialist or symbolic accounts of human cultures. The authors of articles in the *Annual Review of Anthropology* in those years say it all: on the one hand Richard Salisbury (1973), Carol A. Smith (1974), and Harold K. Schneider (1975), and on the other Victor Turner (1975), and Abner Cohen (1979). I experienced the move from the Yale Department of Anthropology to the emerging Johns Hopkins department as immensely liberating. I was freed from the box of "China anthropology," and from the box of "symbolic anthropology."

In some ways the department seemed ahead of its time. While the field of anthropology was reeling from the publication of *Writing culture* (Clifford and Marcus 1986), we wondered what all the fuss was about. From the beginning of its existence, we had built the department on the assumption that the observing anthropologist was part of any ethnography. We were guided by Sid Mintz' (1974) biography of Taso, and by Rich Price's (2002) layered history of Suriname.

When we had a full roster of faculty and began taking graduate students, we decided students would be required to take courses from all of us: the more "materialist" Mintz and Trouillot, and the more "symbolist" Feeley-Harnik, Martin, Price, and Lavendera. Courses and seminars would combine Sid Mintz on Gresham's Law with Gillian Feeley-Harnik on ancestors in Madagascar, or the Africa area expertise of David Cohen with the Caribbean area expertise of Sally and Rich Price. Faculty were expected to teach courses jointly, so from one semester to the next I paired up with Mintz, Verdery, Harvey, Feeley-Harnik, or Ghani. Over the generations, this plan produced many student projects, which cut across the materialist-symbolist divide in unexpected ways, and generally were sensitive to the effect of the observer in the chronicle.[1]

---

1.   See: http://anthropology.jhu.edu/alumni.html

In 1986, this rich potential was still only a promissory note. My own place in the emerging synergy was as a complete novice in Marx's writing and Marxian analysis. I had been socialized by Victor Turner, James Siegel, and Terry Turner at Cornell, and by the more qualitative sides of China scholars Arthur Wolf and G. William Skinner. I had also had a substantial education in Wittgenstein's later thought while still a Cornell graduate student, at the feet of Norman Malcolm, Georg Von Wright, Max Black, and Bruce Goldberg.

THE CLASSICS AND HOW THEY WERE READ

We began the practice of training graduate students through extensive reading of classic works in anthropology and in the history of social thought. Sharing the privilege of teaching this class, often teaching it jointly, was another way beyond anthropology's symbolic and material boxes because the disciplinary divisions that plagued us—between psychology, sociology, history, natural history, and anthropology among others—had not yet been formed at the time these classics were written. I can best give a sense of what was gained by this approach through an example from one of the little known works of these lectures' namesake, Lewis Henry Morgan. Morgan was well known for his evolutionary studies of kinship systems and his advocacy as a lawyer on behalf of Native Americans in upstate New York. But he was also an accomplished student of the natural world. In *The American beaver and his works*, Morgan endeavored to take account of all the actors on the scene: Native Americans, loggers, farmers, fur trappers, railroad employees, engineers, and the beavers themselves. Looking back, this was nothing if not an early project in the anthropology of science. Morgan imagined the beavers' environment through their eyes: their lodges were "as if finished with a mason's trowel" (Morgan 1868: 149); he expresses astonishment at their "mechanical skill" (150). To back up his claim that their construction of canals was done by excavation as "the highest act of intelligence and knowledge" (191), he gathered observations worthy of any fieldworker. He saw that the ends of the roots along the edges of the canal bore teeth marks, and, to prove to himself that the canals were artificially constructed, he demonstrated their use in transporting wood by floating pieces of wood along the length of the canal from its farthest end to the burrow (196).

Through the lens of his beaver studies, Morgan became to me less of an evolutionist mired in the long discredited ideas of the nineteenth century and more of a natural historian, alert to the details of the landscape and the marks various creatures made on it. This was neither biology nor history but something hybrid that could point to the future of an empirical anthropology alert to material constraints, symbolic gestures, and the details of how purposeful activity leaves residues on the environment. When it came time to write my lectures, I was mindful that Chinese house cleaning at new years might be a deeply purposeful rather than a utilitarian mechanical ritual; that rotating credit societies, seemingly illogical because no profit seemed to be produced, might be a creative means for survival in a specific social and historical environment.

Another example in an inspirational text could be Friedrich Engels' writing on the complexity of the family and on the human hand, both in relation to labor. Here is a hint of his lesser-known writing on the human hand:

> Thus the hand is not only the organ of labor, *it is also the product of labor.* Only by labor, by adaptation to ever new operations, by inheritance of the thus acquired special development of muscles, ligaments and, over longer periods of time, bones as well, and by the ever-renewed employment of this inherited finesse in new, more and more complicated operations, has the human hand attained the high degree of perfection that has enabled it to conjure into being the pictures of a Raphael, the statues of a Thorwaldsen, the music of a Paganini. (Engels 1950: 9)

He saw that the apparently separate materiality of the hand as a biological adaptation cannot be separated from the *use* of the hand in human actions. By extension, this meant to me that the female body, used in specific ways in the labor of reproduction, had probably come to be seen as a tool for this labor. In the lectures I was feeling my way toward a view of the contemporary US female body as made by medical forces beyond its control. But also since the woman inside the body instantiated those forces when in labor (for birthing), she might also able to articulate what it is like to be under such control. Thus we might have insider commentary on the relationship between the reproduction of future generations and the reproduction of laborers (Engels and Leacock 1972).

My education in reading *Capital* I owe primarily to David Harvey. Through many readings over the years, I saw the inaccuracy of seeing Marx as a materialist pure and simple. The devil was in the details. I was startled to realize that what Marx meant by "use value" was not a utilitarian notion of something useful for physical survival but "a thing which through its qualities satisfies human needs of whatever kind." He expands: "whether they arise, for example, from the stomach, or the imagination, makes no difference" (Marx 2006: 125). I was indelibly struck that what enabled exchange value to play its part in the commodity, and "labor value" to play its part in value, was the human capacity for "the power of abstraction" (90). Abstraction, I came to see, was a powerful but often invisible process that lay behind our ability to treat coats and boots (made of different materials and by means of different labor skills) seem commensurable on the same scale. Once this kind of commensurability becomes general in a society, "Circulation becomes the great social retort into which everything is thrown, to come out again as the money crystal. Nothing is immune from this alchemy, the bones of the saints cannot withstand it, let alone more delicate . . . consecrated objects" (229). These ideas were at the front of my mind as I tried to understand how the labor of birthing a baby in the US could be organized on the model of the labor that makes commodities. Or as I tried to understand how the principles of a money system could be elaborated into a system of paper tokens used as a calculus of caring for dead relatives in China.

I was led to think about all forms of exchange, equivalences, obligations, and saving in Chinese villages without assuming that they were treated as commodities. One could agree with Marx that, "Just as in money every qualitative difference between commodities is extinguished, so too for its part, as a radical leveler, it extinguishes all distinctions" (ibid.: 229). But one could still ask whether non-commoditized social forms and values might persist alongside commoditized ones. This would mean that not all qualitative differences among things would be extinguished. If qualitative differences did persist in Chinese villages, they could only be understood by reference to deeply held practices and values about kinship, power, inheritance, flourishing—in short the socially defined cosmological order.

When it came to understanding the topic of my fourth lecture, Protestants who were making Wheels of Fortune to attract wealth, I was led to Marx's commodity fetishism, in which producers see the things they produce as "what they are," "material relations between persons and social relations between things" (ibid.: 166). Thus, since things have actually come to have social relations with other things, there is no illogic in trying to attract them to oneself. But I was also led to Weber, who presaged Foucault on the detailed techniques of power that operate in bureaucracies and organized religions. I remembered his clarion call at the end of *The Protestant ethic and the spirit of capitalism*:

> For to the extent that asceticism moved out of the monastic cell, was transferred to the life of work in a vocational calling, and then commenced to rule over this-worldly morality, it helped to construct the powerful cosmos of the modern economic order . . . this cosmos today determines the style of life of all individuals born into it, *not* only those directly engaged in earning a living. This pulsating mechanism does so with overwhelming force. (Weber 1958: 123)

In this light, I could sympathize with the members of the Unity Church I met, performing a kind of disciplined asceticism as they followed the techniques of attracting wealth, and deferred enjoyment to a future time.

With the help of my colleagues and the classics, I had come a long way from the battle between materialism and symbolism. Imagination and survival, style and force, abstraction and commodity: these pairs were not artificial constructions but rather like the beaver canal, a means for anthropologists to comprehend the complexity of culture. Another classic writer we read, Gregory Bateson, summed it up for me, asserting that the world and human experience of the world are entwined: there is not one without the other, despite materialism's effort to exclude mind. As he puts it,

> I suddenly realized that of course the bridge between map and territory is difference. It is only news of difference that can get from the territory to the map, and this fact is the basic epistemological statement about the relationship between all reality out there and all perception in here: that the bridge must always be in the form of difference. Difference,

out there, precipitates coded or corresponding difference in the aggregate of differentiation which we call the organism's mind. And that mind is immanent in matter, which is partly inside the body—but also partly "outside," e.g., in the form of records, traces, and perceptibles (Brockman 2004).

I would look for the traces of mind in matter, so to speak, in ephemera like Chinese paper money burned at funerals, or pictures of commodities pasted on Wheels of Fortune.

THE IMPETUS FOR THE PROJECT

The invitation to give the 1986 Morgan lectures was extended after I had stopped doing regular fieldwork in Chinese villages and before I finished my first ethnographic study about reproductive biology in the US. Caught a bit betwixt and between as far as ethnographic projects were concerned, the lectures became a kind of "applied Johns Hopkins anthropology."

I had done a modest amount of ethnography in an unassuming Methodist church in Baltimore, which held a session on "Prosperity Thought" every Thursday morning. The session included "laying on of hands" faith healing by noted spiritual adept Olga Worrall. Fellow anthropologist Lorna Rhodes and I became regular visitors to the service while I delved into the history of prosperity thought and thought control in American contexts. This, I hoped, could be the justification for an exploration of "symbolic" ideas about money in the context of late capitalism in the US, where the fetishism of the money form reached its apotheosis. Obviously drawing too simple a comparison, but one I hoped would be fertile for thought, I returned to my earlier first hand experience in Chinese villages and historical sources about Chinese ideas and practices concerning measures of value. Before my mind as an organizing object was the wooden rice "measure" the *tau*—a standard volumetric measuring device made of wood and metal, like a small barrel. It was used in a utilitarian way to measure the rice one purchased from the rice merchant. But it was also used as a key object in funeral processions, carried by the eldest son. Inside the *tau* would be 5 grains, standing for nourishment, a handful of nails, standing for sons, and a variety of coins, standing for wealth. What was this object? How could I encapsulate the material meanings it held for people and in the world? Could I bring together the insights from reading the classics and my colleagues to shed light on this densely significant object? Could I write about aspects of American culture's contemporary obsessions with monetary value in a way that would echo Marx's insights about abstraction, or Engels on the leakage of imagined relations of reproduction between different social spheres? Most importantly, could I convey the many instances I experienced doing fieldwork in Chinese villages where exchange, debt, obligation, and transfer of objects of land seemed to work on a logic counter to anything I had experienced at home?

IN THE PRESENT

In 1986 it was impossible to predict the extent to which global capital would continue to invade virtually every aspect of work and life. It was also impossible to imagine that anthropologists would gain a significant voice in public discourse, allowing them to raise objections to this invasion. Recent works by David Graeber and Gillian Tett, for example, have become a pair of readings to die for: Graeber lays out in plain language what makes an obligation and a debt work differently and how money is necessary for debt (Graeber 2011); Tett shows in equally plain language how the credit boom depended on social silence, on what was unsayable yet crucial to unfolding events (Tett 2009: xiii). At the time it was only possible to dream of the detailed ethnographic studies of money and markets around the world that are now on our shelves. Jane Guyer and Sidney Mintz were pioneers in this of course (see especially Mintz 1986; Guyer 1995, 2004), but in due course they were joined by, among others, Ellen Hertz (1998), Karen Ho (2009), Bill Maurer (2011), and most recently Erica Schoenberger (2014). These 1986 Morgan Lectures are a long ago stepping stone along a path since greatly extended by others, but such as they are, they could only have been written with the help of the collective experience of the Johns Hopkins anthropology department.

CHAPTER I

Money and value in China

Here in Upstate New York during the middle of the nineteenth century, there was a Classical revival that inspired people to represent emerging American capitalism in the symbols of the ancient Greek Republic. They named towns Syracuse, Macedon, or Ithaca, and they formed fraternal Greek orders. In the face of this enthusiasm, Lewis Henry Morgan was instrumental in proposing that his fraternal order, "The Gordian Knot," change its name to "The Grand Order of the Iroquois" and reorganize itself along the lines of the League of the Iroquois (White 1959: 3). While many were focusing on the golden age of Greece as a model for American civilization, Morgan was focusing on contemporary groups of Indians, whom he saw not as a part of civilization but as victims of its "dark frauds," "base bribery," and "soulless avarice" (White 1959: 3).

My theme in these lectures, which honor Morgan, begins with his penchant for finding a stance from which to criticize economic processes in his own society by seeing how differently things could work in other societies. While Morgan's criticisms were not as thorough-going as some would like (Bohannan 1967: vi), he did succeed in attaining (at this early date) what I think is one of the most valuable things anthropology has to offer the modern world—a vantage point from which to see the inner logic of our own world by taking on the perspective of other societies constituted by different historical forces.

The difficulty of this change in perspective must not be underestimated. Marx once said that we do not see contradictions in our own society because we feel as much at home among them as a fish in water (1967, III: 729). Even if we do find a way to see the water we are swimming in, how do we manage to attain a critical vision of it without overlooking its advantages? How do we describe societies founded on different principles, the very ones that might help us see the contingent nature of our own, without romanticizing them and failing to see their disadvantages? How do we begin to conceptualize forms of social organization that move beyond both our own and other existing societies? The focus I have chosen for these lectures, namely the meaning of money, contains two major paradoxes. One of these paradoxes concerns money's socially (integrating) function and the other concerns its socially (disintegrating) function. I will introduce both now, but my emphasis in the first two lectures on China will be on the paradox that involves the integrating and (enhancing) of human social interaction. The second paradox will play a greater role in the last two lectures. To begin with the first prong of the first paradox, Marx extolled money's powers as the "God among commodities," the "real community, since it is the general substance of survival for all and at the same time the social product of all" (Colletti 1975: 55). Simmel describes it as "pure interaction in its purest form" (1978: 129), exchange in a "congealed form," "the reification of exchange among people" (1978: 176).

But the other prong of this paradox is that money can lead not toward pure sociability, but toward personal freedom: Simmel sees money as a "magna charta" of personal freedom" (1978: 286). "The lord of the manor who can demand a quantity of beer or poultry or honey from a serf thereby determines the activity of the latter in a certain direction. But the moment he imposes merely a money levy the peasant is free, in so far as he can decide whether to keep bees or cattle or anything else" (1978: 286). Whereas the medieval corporation "embraced the whole individual" (1978: 313), a money economy allows an individual to participate only to a limited degree in an association: "Money has made it possible for people to join a group without having to give up any personal freedom and reserve" (1978: 344). As a modern commentator has put it, the community of money tends to be "strongly marked by individualism and certain conceptions of liberty, freedom, and equality backed by laws of private property, rights to appropriation, and freedom of contract"

(Harvey 1985: 4). In sum, the first paradox is that money leads toward (both) enhanced social exchange (and) enhanced personal freedom.

The second paradox, briefly here, points to aspects of money that are inimical to human interaction and potentiality. Money has been held to produce the "blasé attitude," feelings of greyness about everything, because it measures everything from groceries to virtue in the same coin. Money has also been held to replace social relationships, substituting itself in our thinking for relations among people.

The other side of the second paradox is that, instead of producing greyness, confusion, and feelings of moral uncertainty, money can also produce the most intense, clear, and passionately directed feelings, especially toward the accumulation of more of itself. Innumerable commentators have remarked on the vice of avarice and the evils of greed, none more vividly than the early Protestant commentators on usury. Describing the seventeenth-century illustration in Figure 1, Blaxton compares the usurer to the pig:

Figure 1. Blaxton, *The English Usurer*. Title page illustration.

> The Covetous wretch, to what may we compare,
>   better than Swine: both of one nature are,
> One grumbles, the other grunts: both grosse, and dull,
>   hungry, still feeding, and yet never full.
> Resemblance from their habits may be had,
>   the one in furre, th'other in Bristles clad.
> (Blaxton 1634: A2)

And in his commentary he adds:

> The Usurer is like a Pigge, for while he liveth, he is good, and profitable
> for nothing, for he will be ever rooting up the earth: running thorough,
> and tearing of hedges: eating and devouring up good Corne, Beanes and
> Peason: so likewise doth the wicked swinish Usurer while hee liveth: but
> then the Pigge is dead, then there commeth profit by him to many; so
> the Usurer, when death taketh him, then the poore may have some profit.
> (Blaxton 1634: 47)

In sum, in the second paradox, money both confuses our perceptions of the interactions on which society is based and leads us into clearly conceived but socially harmful pursuits.

It is clear that money can perform its socially integrating and socially disintegrating functions at the same time. Both Marx and Simmel saw this. Simmel said: "Money simultaneously exerts both a disintegrating and a unifying effect" (1978: 345). And Marx concurs: "If money is the bond which ties me to human life and society to me, which links me to nature and to man, is money not the bond of all bonds? Can it not bind and loose all bonds? Is it therefore not the universal means of separation? It is the true agent of separation and the true cementing agent, it is the chemical power of society" (1975: 377).

The overall picture, summarized in Figure 2, has two parts. On the one hand, at the top of the diagram, we can think of money flowing throughout a society, moving from hands to hands, creating webs of exchange and enhancing social interaction. At the same time, it para-doxically creates possibilities of personal freedom, as it empowers indi-viduals to spend their money in ways of their own choosing. These are the aspects of money that can help integrate us together in society. On the other hand, at the bottom of the diagram, we can think of money creating feelings of indifference: when it becomes the measure of all things, it undermines our ability to discriminate one thing from another. And paradoxically, it can also become the focus of intense desire and greed. These are the aspects of money that can help split us apart and increase the disintegration of society. My two cases, China and the United States, relate to the diagram in this way: money in Chinese society works mostly, but not entirely, to create social integration; money in the United States works mostly, but not entirely, to create social disintegration.

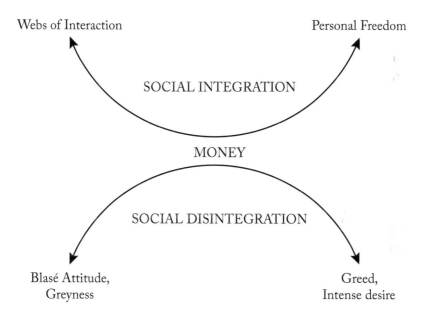

Figure 2. The movements of money.

To begin to think with me about these factors, consider a series of transactions of increasing complexity, with no implication that this series actually occurred historically. Begin with barter, transactions often found in our society among our children. My daughter offers one of the stickers in her collection, a "puffy," of which she has many, to her friend in exchange for an "oily," of which she has few. A minimal amount of trust is involved in this transaction. Assuming each child can examine the stickers and be sure they are genuine, there is no felt need for any particular reliance on the trustworthiness of the other because barter is a "one-off affair," it entails no further transactions (Humphrey 1985: 51). Slightly more complex is delayed barter, where my daughter gives away her sticker today, trusting that her friend will bring another of equivalent value tomorrow. Here there has to be trust and probably prior knowledge of the person's character (Humphrey 1985: 52).

When money is exchanged for goods, the transaction seems a little like barter in that it can be simultaneous, so that trust in the other person is not necessary. But money is socially denser than barter in two ways. First, to reap the benefit of the money you pay me, I must make a further payment, and so on. Money has a tendency to circulate indefinitely (Crump 1981: 3–4). Second, like delayed barter, money entails social bonds, but even wider ones. Acceptance of money depends on "confidence in the ability of an economic community [a state, say] to ensure that the value given in exchange for an interim value, a coin, will be replaced without loss" (Simmel 1978: 178).

It follows from the ability of money to be many things at once that, in and of itself, it does not necessarily either enhance and create or diminish and destroy human relationships. Consequently, it can enter a traditional society, thick with face-to-face social relationships and based on trust and reciprocity, without destroying it. Sometimes it can be held within certain spheres of exchange (Gregory 1980: 649); other times it can be "tamed" for social purposes. My overall argument in the first two lectures is that in China the way money articulates with forms of exchange based on kinship and community has held the distintegrating potential of money in check. In lectures 3 and 4, I will follow out the consequences of money's second paradox. To anticipate, in our own society's relative lack of the integument of social custom, the distintegrating effects of money loom large. Even when we extoll the accumulation of money as a way of attempting to collect the social trust on which it depends, this is a mirage, in which the abstract form of social exchange is mistaken for its living substance (Nelson 1949: 135).

Let me start with a brief look at the ethnographic contexts I will be considering. The two lectures on China will focus on contemporary Taiwan, where I did fieldwork during several trips between 1969 and 1975. Taiwan was a province of China during the last dynasty, the Ch'ing (1644–1912), became a Japanese colony from 1895 to 1945, and is now an independent state. Because the ancestors of the Chinese people I lived with came from southeastern China two hundred years ago, I will occasionally dip into accounts of travellers, missionaries, photographers, and ethnographers from nineteenth- and early-twentieth-century China. For comparison I will also make some reference to the People's Republic of China (PRC), which has been a socialist society since 1949. For the United States I will use various historical materials, some contemporary fieldwork I have done in Baltimore, Maryland, and some materials from the mass media.

The justification for constructing this particular comparison (China and the United States) is primarily that these are the countries in which I have done fieldwork. But there are two other reasons. First, they are tied together through the man these lectures honor, Lewis Henry Morgan. Morgan deeply influenced the Chinese Marxist historian Kuo Mo-jo, whose studies were widely published in China in the 1930s (Dirlik 1978: 137–40). When I traveled in China in 1984, a half-century later, as a member of a delegation of anthropologists and sociologists, we heard many lectures from our Chinese counterparts at academic gatherings, in which they used Morgan's evolutionary schemes to account for the marriage and kinship systems of China's minorities. Second, in both countries money seems to be a topic which people find utterly engrossing. Because I believe it is engrossing for quite different reasons in the two countries, the contrast helps me shed light on the subject.

In *Ancient Society*, Morgan made a basic distinction between two kinds of societies, which he called *societas* and *civitas*. In *civitas*, the division of labor is highly developed and property relationships (private ownership of land and resources) come to have a "controlling influence," "dominating as a passion over all other passions" (Morgan 1877: 6). I will try to show that even though China and the United States are both state societies with highly developed markets, they fall on opposite sides of Morgan's distinction between *societas* and *civitas*: in China human and personal relations dominate and determine property relations, whereas in the United States property relations dominate and determine the nature of human relations—in Morgan's words, they occupy a "commanding force in the human mind" (1877: 527).

Let me begin with a brief sketch of money and exchange in Chinese history. In China, exchange of commodities at markets and the development of money commodities are very ancient. Coins and bullion circulated as a medium of exchange from as early as the fourth and third centuries BC (Yang 1952: 1–2). By Han times (206 BC–AD 220), a round bronze coin with a square hole in the middle was the standard medium for ordinary transactions. (Coins in the same general form continued in circulation for more than two thousand years, until the end of the Ch'ing dynasty in 1912 [Yang 1952: 2]. Figure 3 shows some I bought in an antique shop.) Figure 4 is a depiction of an early Han market at which

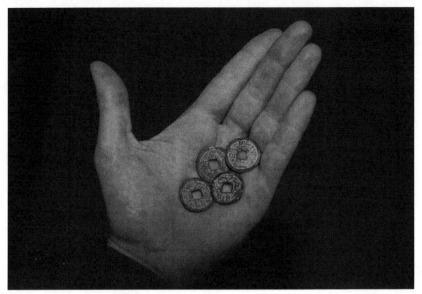

Figure 3. Chinese coins. Photo by the author.

Figure 4. Market in the early Han dynasty (206 BCE–220 CE).

similar coins would have been used. As a means of payment in large transactions, various forms of money commodities were used over time. Strong
dynasties operated with gold and silver and even issued paper money from
the eleventh century on, as in the Ming paper bill shown in Figure 5.

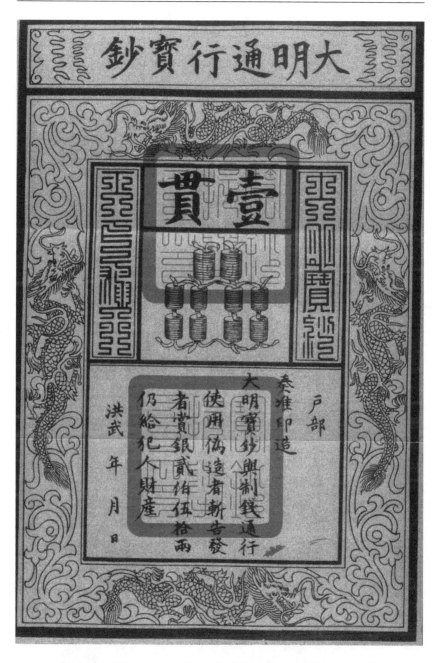

Figure 5. Paper money from the Ming dynasty (1368–1644).

Throughout the premodern period, there was a steady increase in the number and density of markets at which currency could be spent, both those focused on urban settlements of permanent shops and periodic markets that depended in large part on itinerant craftsmen and peddlers. In Figure 6 we see some nineteenth-century craftsmen and peddlers: from the left a Kiangsi soup vendor, fortune teller, barber, and wood turner. In Figure 7 there is is a Hong Kong physician touting his wares. And in Figure 8 there is a twentieth-century counterpart, an itinerant pepper grinder, from Shanghai.

Figure 6. Nineteenth-century vendors and craftsmen from Kiangsi province.

Given the length of time Chinese have been marketing commodities and issuing currencies, many, including Max Weber and Mao Tse-tung, have wondered whether, by the end of the last dynasty, China had developed at least the rudiments, the sprouts, of capitalism. Without worrying over the definition of sprouts, it is by now clear (at least in broad terms) what the shape of late traditional Chinese society was like, and it is important for what follows that we see how it was not a fully blown capitalist system. Since ancient times, the official philosophy and policy of status rankings went in the order, from top to bottom: scholar-official,

Figure 7. Nineteenth-century Hong Kong physician selling his wares.

Figure 8. Itinerant pepper grinder in Shanghai in the 1980s. Photo by the author.

peasant, artisan, and merchant. Scholars, laboring with their minds, were most highly valued (Figure 9). Peasants, who produced wealth on which the whole nation depended for sustenance, were valued next, shown in Figure 10 sieving rice in contemporary Taiwan. Artisans, as secondary producers of wealth, came next: in Figure 11 we see a shoemaker and a blacksmith. And merchants as middle men, such as the tea dealers in Figure 12, who "depended on squeezing a profit from [their] fellow human beings" (Loewe 1968: 152), were ranked last (Ho 1964: 41–42). These rankings had practical consequences: up until the end of the Sung period (960–1279), "the law forbade artisans and merchants and their families to take government examinations" (Ho 1964: 41), the main route to official prestige and power (Twitchett 1968: 68). Figure 13 shows the individual cells in which the examinations were taken. In addition, merchants were separated from officialdom by elaborate sumptuary laws that governed what they could eat or wear, and how large or ornate their houses could be (Ch'u 1962; Twitchett 1968: 67). In reality, merchants were often able to circumvent these restrictions, as illustrated in Figure 14 (Ho 1964: 42), but the overall effect was to prevent the emergence of a bourgeoisie in the Western sense. Wealthy merchants, and they could be very wealthy, spent a large percentage of their accumulated riches trying to emulate the official elite, scholar-officials. The fabulously prosperous salt merchants of Yang-chou in the eighteenth century, despite heavy taxation of their wealth, "indulged in eccentricities and expensive hobbies, 'dogs, horses, music, and women'; they owned beautiful pleasure gardens; they became bibliophiles, collectors, and art connoisseurs" (Balazs 1964: 52; see also Ho 1964 and Dirlik 1982: 114).

Figure 9. Nineteenth-century scholars.

Figure 10. Sieving rice in Taiwan. Photo by the author.

Figure 11. Nineteenth-century shoemaker and blacksmith.

Figure 12. Nineteenth-century tea dealers.

Figure 13. Nineteenth-century individual cells for the governmental examinations.

Figure 14. Merchants wearing furs and silk.

When merchants did invest wealth rather than spend it, their preferred asset was farm land, and this was so even when urban investment promised greater profits (Balazs 1964: 52; Rawski 1972: 123) (Figure 15). Land may have been regarded as a secure investment, or a prestigious one, but it was not treated, as it often is in our society, as a means of maximizing returns. Rents were often held at a constant amount, and decisions related to production were left up to the tenant (Rawski 1972). Merchant owners were not using "capital" to "transform the nature of agricultural production" (Dirlik 1982: 114). The state had a heavy hand in controlling economic activity when it did arise. As Balazs has put it, "Any sign of initiative in the [merchant] camp was usually strangled at birth, or if it had reached a stage when it could no longer be suppressed, the state laid hands on it, took it under control, and appropriated the resultant profits" (1964: 41).

Figure 15. Aerial view of terraced rice fields.

A requirement for the operation of capitalism is that laborers, without other means of livelihood, meet employers in a labor market, where their labor is bought and sold for a wage. There clearly was wage labor in China, but this does not mean there was a "systematic tendency toward the creation of wage labor" (Dirlik 1982: 114). "Production by wage labor still constituted only a minor part of agrarian production. Well into the twentieth century, the predominant form of agrarian production in China continued to be small-scale household production, with the peasant family as the unit both of production and consumption" (1982: 115). For capitalism to flourish, two conditions must coexist: workers must offer their labor to others for a wage, and those to whom they offer it must so control land and other resources that the worker is compelled to sell his labor in order to eat (Eric Wolf 1981: 47–48). In China there were customary impediments to the sale of land. Land inherited from the ancestors was regarded as an estate held in trust by the family head. He did not own it as an individual, nor could he sell it on his own (Sung 1981: 365–66). In a real sense the land was not separate as an alienable thing from the kin group which tilled it. Land and family formed a virtually inseparable unit.

The family could also combine agricultural production with cottage industry without creating the conditions for capitalism (Dirlik 1982: 115). And although merchants might be involved in investing in such industry, they rarely organized it directly, "rather they would coordinate a multiplicity of small producers" (Elvin 1975: 103), like the silk reelers in Figure 16 and the Shanghai embroiderers in Figure 17.

Figure 16. Nineteenth-century silk reelers.

Figure 17. Nineteenth-century embroiderers.

One lesson should be drawn from this sketch of late traditional China: elements of a capitalist economy can exist without implying that the whole system of capitalism as we know it is present. As Arif Dirlik puts it, "What are sprouts of capitalism in one place are not sprouts in another" (1982: 124). This lesson applies equally to Taiwan, even though it is held out by anthropologists and development economists alike as the success story of world capitalism. Certainly as an anthropologist living in a rural area an hour south of the capital city, it was easy to imagine I was witnessing the development of a capitalist economy, commonplace as it was to see and hear about wage labor in factories or shops, bank loans, businesses starting and failing, calculations of monetary wealth on every hand, and endless talk of profit and loss. Even the somewhat arcane ritual symbolism I was mostly interested in at first had money right in the middle of it, as in the mixture of the five grains, money, and nails (representing sons) that is carried in the funeral procession in a wooden rice measure (Figure 18). In the funeral procession, the rice measure is held by the eldest son (Figure 19) and its contents are thrown out over graves to let the ancestors know specifically what their descendants desire.

Figure 18. The five grains in a rice measure in Taiwan. Photo by the author.

Yet amidst these forms that seemed very familiar were others that mystified me. Take, as one among many examples, the practices surrounding the celebration of Chinese New Year. I could understand how it would be important for all members of the household to spend this time together, often traveling long distances from jobs elsewhere to be sure of this (Feuchtwang 1974: 114). I could also understand the sending off of the kitchen gods to heaven—one is pictured behind the stove in Figure 20 and in close-up in Figure 21—so these earthly subordinates in the hierarchy of gods could report to their superiors in heaven on the conduct of household members in the past year. To ensure a good report, the mouth of the paper image of the kitchen god would be smeared with sweet rice (in the old days it was opium) before this paper image was dispatched by burning to the realm of the gods. But I was puzzled by the emphasis around New Years on settling debts. Was this a counterpart in the economic realm of cleaning out the house and washing all the bedding and furniture that we see occurring during the New Year period in Figure 22? Was it imperative that all debts be settled? Why the urgency?

Figure 19. The eldest son holding the rice measure in Taiwan. Photo by the author.

Figure 20. Kitchen god behind the stove in Fukien province. Photo by the author.

Figure 21. Close-up of image of kitchen god in Fukien province. Photo by the author.

Figure 22. New Year's house cleaning in Taiwan. Photo by the author.

Looking back to nineteenth-century accounts of money at New Years only raised more questions. One observer makes it plain that borrowing and lending must come due at New Years:

> Each separate individual is engaged in the task of trying to chase down the men who owe money to him, and compel them to pay up, and at the same time in trying to avoid the persons who are struggling to track him down, and corkscrew from him the amount of his indebtedness to them! The dodges and subterfuges to which each is obliged to resort, increase in complexity and number with the advance of the season until at the close of the month, the national activity is at fever heat. (Smith 1970: 155)

Another describes the strength of the social custom:

> It is universally regarded as a great disgrace not to be able to pay one's debts on the last day of a year. The law does not require debts to be paid at this time, but established custom requires it and the demands of custom are more inexorable and authoritative than the voice of the law. . . . The debtor would not be trusted during the following year unless he paid up his debts in the present. He would be known as a man who did not pay his accounts at the end of a year. . . . His reputation would be ruined. (Doolittle 1865, II: 86–87)

If the sanctions forcing debtors to pay off their debts by New Years were so strong, the urgency of the creditors seems unreasonably great:

> After daylight on the morning of New Year's, [a creditor] occasionally may be seen going about the streets in search of [his debtor] with a lighted lantern in one hand and his account in the other. He does not recognize or admit the fact that it is daylight. With him it is still dark, and in proof of this he carries his lantern, with which to see his way while in pursuit of his delinquent customer. According to custom, he may still pursue his debtor [only] if he carries a lighted lantern, as he would be obliged to carry one were it indeed night. (Doolittle 1865, II: 88)

The assumptions behind the practice? "If a debt is not secured then, it will go over till a new year, and no one knows what will be the status of a claim which has actually contrived to cheat the annual Day of Judgment" (Smith 1970: 155). What kind of debts are these that dissolve unless collected by the "rounding of the year"? This one practice, whose logic is so foreign to our own way of using money, can serve as a loud warning bell that the presence of money itself tells us little about how it will be used. What we must do is examine empirically the wide social context in which money moves around Chinese communities.

I will attempt to do just this in the rest of my talk tonight, focusing on three contexts: labor, marriage, and rotating credit societies. In each case we will see practices that look at first like our own "earning money," "buying things," "making profit," or "investing capital." But in each case, when we have exposed the inner logic of these practices, we will see that money is not being used in ways we might assume: these practices may appear to be sprouts of capitalism at the very least, but I will argue that they are not. Money circulates in Chinese communities in ways premised on an entirely different logic than that of capitalism: it concentrates on the first paradox we discussed earlier, building pure interaction and allowing personal liberty at the same time.

We begin with labor. That hallmark of capitalism, wage labor, is certainly present in Taiwan, for example for those workers who put together the components of our finest stereo systems and the seams of our designer clothes. Yet what people do with these wages has a very unfamiliar look. By and large all members of the family that shares a stove are expected to pool their wages by turning them over to the household head, receiving in return an allowance deemed adequate to meet necessary cash expenses (bus fare, lunch, etc.). It is not that there are never conflicts over these arrangements—there often are. But the general principle is: no "individual" profit, rather collective accumulation out of which individuals receive a share according to need. In this way, even money tainted, so to speak, by capitalist relations of production in factories in which labor is broken down into minute portions and measured and paid by strict time-keeping can be brought within the sphere of family time (Hareven 1982).

How much more should this be so for money paid for labor done within a single village, which escaped the kinds of measures of efficiency and productivity that were characteristic of factory work. The usual rural unit of labor was the "kung," which means the amount of labor one person does in one day, whether transplanting seedlings or harvesting rice. There were wide variations in starting and ending times, number of breaks, intensity of effort, and productivity (Fei and Chang 1948: 30–31). These were not things the employer had it within his power to control, in contrast to a modern factory. The employer–laborer relationship was to some extent a relationship between whole persons. If work was not strictly controlled, neither was it strictly limited: laborers could be ordered to do errands, child care, or other household tasks (Su and Lun 1978: 210). Neither was payment limited to a standard "kung"/money ratio. Meals were expected in addition to wages (Fei and Chang 1948: 32; Su and Lun 1978: 210). In Taiwan it was customary to provide five meals a day to rice harvesters like those in Figure 23, in addition to the day's wage. Although there might be a general supposition that better pay or meals ought to produce better work, what that better work consisted in (faster? more thorough? longer hours?) could not be strictly controlled by the employer. One paid what one could and hoped for the best.

Figure 23. Rice harvesting in Taiwan. Photo by the author.

A current Taiwan case described by Sung Lung-sheng illustrates how money was absorbed by the family, whether its source was the factory or the village:

> The three generation extended Cheng family was headed by Cheng Piao, who was then 70 years old. He and his wife had seven married sons and 40 grandchildren. The family was dispersed in three separate houses. . . . There was a stove in each of these houses, so each residential group constituted a commensal unit. The three wives in the first house rotated cooking responsibilities on a five-day cycle, as did the three wives in the second house. The inhabitants of the third house ate by themselves. . . . [Everyone's] rice came from the family store house, and their vegetables came from the family garden. Cheng Piao went grocery shopping every day, and delivered meat, fish and other foods and necessities to each house on a per capita basis. He also controlled the income from the family's land and knitting machines. . . . His first son was a part-time bricklayer in the vicinity, and his second son was a foreman in a coal mine and the manager of a small variety store. All the money these sons earned was handed over to Cheng. At the end of each year, Cheng gave a sum of money for new clothes and shoes to each according to the numbers and ages of the children in each. He also paid all marriage and educational expenses. (Sung 1981: 368–69)

In sum, although labor may be done in the private relationship of a wage earner to an employer, the money so earned can be pooled into a collective sum of common substance. This raises a question about the identities of the persons involved. Do they see themselves as private, separate independent selves coming together in a contractual arrangement, or do they see their common membership in a collectivity as constitutive of their personhood?

A Japanese scholar, Shuzo Shiga, has explicated traditional Chinese concepts of personhood, by which "during the father's lifetime the son's personality is absorbed into the father's, while after the latter's death his personality is absorbed into that of his son. Father and son are a continuum of the same personality, not two beings in mutual rivalry" (1978: 119–20). For this reason, it was no accident that the classics speak of father and son as "one body (I t'i)" or one breath (I ch'i)" (1978: 122). These old notions seem to bespeak the lack of an isolatable private self; instead they speak to a personhood constituted by membership in a common kin group. I know of no systematic examination of whether this has changed dramatically in modern Taiwan. My own field experience indicates it has not. For example, people commonly referred the cause of bodily illness to discord in the kin group. One day my assistant said she was sick. Thinking she meant she felt physically ill, I offered medicine and a trip to the doctor. She did mean she felt sick, but it was because her father and brothers had quarreled. Because her personhood was constituted by membership in the family, discord in the social "body" had to mean discord in hers.

At this point we have seen that debts, wages, labor, and personhood in contemporary Taiwan are not defined as they would be in a fully capitalist system: they are more like plants of another variety than sprouts of capitalism. Keeping in mind these hints about the logic of money and how it functions in China, let us move on to the exchanges of goods, money, and people involved in marriage and, second, exchange of goods and money in rotating credit societies.

First, then, a look at marriage. How do families that figure descent only through males obtain a wife for a son? In particular is there any sense in which the money and goods transferred from the groom's family to the bride's family at the engagement and wedding should literally be regarded as a "bride price," as China anthropologists have often claimed they should be? Is she being bought by one family and sold by the other? It is clear that unless stringently legislated otherwise, as it was for a time in the PRC, the usual pattern is for an exchange of goods and money to accompany the bride transfer. What happens is that gifts of clothing, jewelry, special cakes, and pork, together with a substantial amount of cash, are sent to the bride's family for the engagement ceremony. In Figure 24 goods are carried on open trays in Taiwan. In Figure 25 they are piled up in front of the bride's house, and in Figure 26 behind the bride. Money in the form of paper bills is displayed openly on trays just as other goods are. At the wedding itself, the money sent by the groom is used up in its entirety to buy the dowry: household furnishings, cloth, clothing, and jewelry for the bride.

Figure 24. Gifts being brought to the bride in Taiwan. Photo by the author.

Figure 25. Gifts to the bride in Taiwan. Photo by the author.

Figure 26. A bride with gifts arranged behind her in Taiwan. Photo by the author.

Most Taiwan villagers I asked asserted that if things work out this way it cannot be considered buying and selling the bride. One said, "In a sense we do expend goods to buy the bride. But, no matter how much we give, we still owe a debt to her parents and grandparents for giving birth to her. If it weren't for them, she would never have existed." The inextricable connections between a woman and the bodies, lives, and efforts of her family do not allow her whole being to be compensated by a single payment, no matter how large. It was only when people imagined what would happen if the usual exchanges failed to take place that they spoke of buying and selling. If the bride's family sends fewer goods with her than the bride price would buy, it is called "taking money from people"; if a bride comes from a very poor family that sends no dowry, it is called "buying" her (Rubie S. Watson 1985: 131). Or if the groom is flawed in some way, talk of buying and selling can enter. My landlady said there was no hope of arranging a regular marriage for her son because he had been in prison and was already thirty-nine years old. "The girl's family can demand as much money as they want for an engagement fee, let them just make money off of it, and our family will pay. They won't have to send a dowry at all. We will just buy a daughter-in-law."

I think it is plain that a marriage with the full panoply of rites and exchanges, where neither partner has been married before, is not thought of as a market transaction in which one party profits. The term for such an ideal marriage is *Ming-mei jeng-ch'u*: "taking in marriage in a beautiful and correct way." The term used for "taking in marriage" in this phrase is *ch'u*. It differs by only one element—the female radical—from the homophone *ch'u*, and this homophone's meaning has to do with choice and movement in space. Another main term used in referring to marriage is a classic performative like "promise," where one's actions and words in and of themselves constitute a change in status. The term is *tso*, and it means "to make, to be, to act as, to do." In the phrase *Tso sim-pu* it means to "make a daughter-in-law" or betroth a girl to one's son. Terms for the goods that move back and forth also carry no implication of monetary recompense or profit. *P'ing-chin*, "engagement gold," is the term for all the goods sent to the bride's family and its basic meaning is to "invite by presents." What is stressed is the necessity for a prior relationship to be established between two families if a major marriage is to occur. Thus the phrase *P'ing tse wei ch'i* means "one cannot become a legal wife except by betrothal exchanges."

In contrast to all this is the term I have translated "buy," used when the bride's family sends too small a dowry or none at all. This term in Taiwanese is *khit* (Mandarin *ch'i*) and its dictionary meaning is not to "buy" but to "beg or entreat." Its sense, I think, is that the usual relationship of roughly equal social standing between affines is missing, and one side or the other is greatly socially subordinate, because of bad behavior (my landlord's son had been in prison) or serious poverty. What is happening in ideal marriages is that rights in the woman are being transferred from one family to another—rights in sex, reproduction, and labor. The money and goods that move to and fro establish a literal connection where one may well never have existed before, they allow both families to display their wealth, and they endow the bride with the material basis of her conjugal unit. This was so even when, until it was ended by law in 1949, China carried on a large market for the buying and selling of human beings: children for adoption or slaves; women for secondary wives, concubines, or slaves (James L. Watson 1980). One Hong Kong man objected to the possibility that a girl purchased as a child and intended to marry a son of the family could ever be considered a major wife: "How can a little daughter-in-law . . . be a proper major wife if you buy her like a piglet in the market?" (James L. Watson 1980: 244). But in marked contrast, major wives were not "bought," they were "brought" into marriage (1980: 241, 232).

Further evidence that marriage gifts are different from market purchases is that when women's monetary contribution to the family goes up, as it has in both Taiwan and the PRC, there is no corresponding proportional rise in the bride "price" in relation to dowry. In 1985 Margery Wolf found "no evidence that this increased 'value' for women has been expressed in bride prices . . . bride price and dowry are both present and . . . have increased at an equal rate. I have no doubts about the uses to which the bride price was put: it was plowed back into the dowry, and parents claimed much more was added besides" (1985: 179).

So far I have spoken of the movement of goods and money back and forth between the affines as if its job were to open a road of interaction between them. In speaking of gift exchange in New Guinea, Gregory describes how

Gifts of high rank create major "highways" that connect people of high rank, gifts of low rank create minor by-ways that connect people of low rank, while middle ranking gifts connect the highways and by-ways to form an extremely complicated network for roads complete with major junctions, minor junctions, fly-overs, roundabouts, one-way avenues and cul-de-sacs. (1982: 57–58)

In a sense Chinese marriage includes gifts of all degrees of importance, from pigs and gold to candy and small amounts of cash, which taken together open a thoroughfare between the new affines. The fathers of the groom and the bride are hosted by the groom at a feast several days after the wedding: it is the gift exchange that creates affinity, for once the initial engagement gifts have been accepted, neither the bride's family nor she herself can back out.

Money and goods move back and forth between families, opening roads of interaction. Some of this money and one substance in particular—gold—seem to distill out of exchange. These distillates capture the two sides of the money paradox we began with, because they both are pure embodiments of exchange and, as we will see, enable personal liberty. As such they are altogether unlike the "profit" that distills out of the circulation of money in capitalism. The first precipitate is a fund of cash that belongs to the bride. It would usually be made up of gifts from friends, a portion of the engagement fee, or a portion of the bride's inheritance from her natal family (Cohen 1976: 170). This money is the woman's private fund, and can be used as she wishes, to buy special things for her children, to invest (Cohen 1976: 180), or to keep as a secret emergency fund (1976: 178). It stands as a reminder of the woman's shared identity with another family, and as a marker of her separation from her husband's family. Separate in substance as a product of an unrelated man's seed, she and others like her are the only ones in Chinese families who have privately controlled wealth (McAleavy 1955: 546; Shiga 1978: 118; Freedman 1979b: 258).

The second precipitate of the marriage exchange besides cash may be a store of gold. This gold, in the form of jewelry—earrings, rings, hair ornaments—usually comes in part from the groom's engagement gifts (James L. Watson 1980: 231; Rubie S. Watson 1985: 129). Unlike the wedding cash, which the bride might spend or invest, this gold was treated as treasure. The ornaments might be worn on special occasions, but they would ordinarily be locked in the bride's top dresser drawer and they would not be sold unless she was desperate.

I think that this golden precipitate of exchange has to be understood in part as an emulation of state power and status. For centuries in imperial China only the central government could legitimately accumulate gold and silver in its treasury. Hoarding gold, taking it out of circulation in this way, was necessary to anticipate future expenses, since there was no notion of deficit financing (Yang 1952: 4–5). Similarly, elaborate sumptuary laws limited the wearing of gold ornaments and other precious metals and jewels to officialdom. As late as the Ch'ing dynasty, "Women of the common people could possess only one gold hair ornament and one pair of gold earrings" (Ch'u 1965: 141). In Taiwan, small god's temples, like the one for the earth god shown in Figure 27, or large ones, like the one in Figure 28, are modeled on a nineteenth-century official's *Yamen*—his place of business and residence. Ancestral hall roofs are decorated and shaped in a way prohibited to commoners but allowed officials in the Ch'ing dynasty (Figure 29). Given the continuing resonance with nineteenth-century marks of prestige, it should be no surprise that gold would be treasured in the locked drawer of a bride's dowry dresser as a sign of her family's status and power.

The final resting place of such gold might well be the grave, if the woman chose to be buried in her ornaments. As an aside that will be important later, bones are generally another sort of lasting gold-like residue of human activity. In parts of southeastern China and Taiwan, several years after death, a specialist is hired to collect up all the bones of the deadout of the grave, organize them, and place them in a ceramic urn. A specialist is hired to collect up all the bones, organize them, and place them in the urn (Figure 30). Family members, including women, rub away the fleshy residue on the bones and clean out the skull (Figure 31). This preserves the bones and allows them to be moved about as descendants try to capture good geomantic forces that will bring them sons, wealth, and peace. It is surely no accident that the urns are called "gold pots" and that the bones in a good geomantic location are said to glow softly within.

Figure 27. Village earth god temple in Taiwan. Photo by the author.

Figure 28. Large temple in Taiwan. Photo by the author.

Figure 29. Ancestral hall in Taiwan. Photo by the author.

Figure 30. Collecting the ancestral bones in an urn in Taiwan. Photo by the author.

Figure 31. Cleaning the ancestral bones in Taiwan. Photo by the author.

Gold acts as a precipitate of exchange, an embodiment of value. Gold ornaments are buried with the bones, and the golden "bone pots" are meant to last in the grave forever. Money, in contrast, continues its role as road-opener, circulator, even after death, and between the living and the dead. In a dramatic illustration of this, it is still customary in present-day Taiwan, as it was in the nineteenth century, to suspend a coin from strings attached to the coffin so that the coin hangs for a time in the mouth of the corpse. After the coin is withdrawn, it is presented to the eldest son of the deceased, who "treasures this coin, and hangs it on his neck as an amulet" (Dore 1966: 47). As money moves between the dead and the living, and between affines, we see how it represents "congealed exchange," pure interaction. We have also had a glimpse of its personally liberatory aspect, as it gives women their own private wealth.

The last context in which I will examine exchange and the circulation of money from person to person is the rotating credit society. Called *hui* in Chinese, this institution is documented for almost all parts of traditional China and flourishes today in Taiwan, Hong Kong, and among overseas Chinese. Although these societies have been seen by anthropologists as sprouts of capitalism, "proto-banks," with which peasants learned the credit arrangements and manipulations of money made necessary in capitalism, I will argue that money circulated in them in ways premised on an entirely different logic than that of capitalism, the same logic, in fact, that we saw money followed in marriage: building pure interaction and allowing personal liberty at the same time.

First let us look at the range of variation in the forms credit associations take. At the simplest end is a kind of rotating pool of money made up of contributions from the members of a club and shared by each of them in turn. A more complex version builds in the principle that those who take the money soonest pay more and those who take it last pay less. As this was described to me in Taiwan, in a $50 group, every member—say there are nine—contributes $50 to the head at its first meeting, for a total of $450. At every meeting afterward, there is a bidding for who will take the pot. The member who bids the highest figure is saying he is willing to pay this amount for the privilege of taking the money at that meeting. Say on the second meeting the highest bid is $10. This bidder then gets a full $50 from the head, and $50 minus his bid of $10 or $40 from the eight others for a total of $370. As meetings go by, the number of members paying in the full $50 would increase each time. Overall, the first several bidders appear to be paying interest, and the last several appear to be receiving it. However, I would like to argue the participants may not have seen it this way at all.

To understand how they did see it, we first have to realize how the movement of money from member to member in these groups depended on a history of good faith and trust. As Fei and Chang observed in the mid-twentieth century, "The functioning of this system depends on the invariable discharge of their obligations by the subscribers, and this is secured only by existing ties of friendship and kinship" (1948: 120–21). Yet the ties of kinship people preferred may not include their closest ones. Fei and Chang found that villagers tended to join societies with friends and affinal relatives (through marriage) rather than patrilineal kin. They comment that close agnatic relatives should assist one without "such special devices" (1948: 120). Since close agnates like brothers are bound by their common substance to a shared identity, one brother demanding payment from another was seen as impossible (Fei 1939: 267).

The same went for more distant agnates: "We were acquainted with a man who complained bitterly because his uncle was insisting that he pay his assessment on time. Kinship ties are built on the principle of mutual help, and it is not well to attempt to exploit them in ordinary business transactions" (Fei and Chang 1948: 121). The corporate nature of the kinship group does not allow individuated interests to form. In contrast, money in its personally liberatory aspects is at work in rotating credit societies. Both women, who had no right to that estate, and sons, whose fathers would not be likely to give them a portion of the patrimonial estate for a personal reason, could accumulate funds through rotating credit societies. In fact, one frequently hears querulous remarks from anthropologists that women dominate these institutions: Myron Cohen found that fully 25 percent of the members of the societies in his village were women (1976: 181). And of course, the money they invest is often precisely their private hoard of wedding cash.

But is the money men and women invest in these societies seen as leading to profit at someone else's expense? Gregory makes a key point about different types of accumulation. There is the accumulation we are accustomed to in capitalism $(m-m')$ in which money seems to make more money, and in which the accumulation can go on indefinitely. But there is another kind of accumulation in which the "prime" is not seen as profit, but rather is seen as creating an obligation to engage in another interaction at a later time (Gregory 1982: 53). In the later interaction, of course, the "prime" may circulate on to someone else within the same community, and so not lead to any one person accumulating more than anyone else. As in the illustration above, if in gift exchange, A gives B $100 and later receives back $110, the additional $10 creates an obligation for A to continue the gift exchange. In contrast, in a capitalist system, the increment of $10 finishes off the transaction, because it is regarded as interest, or payment for the use of the original $100 over time.

In the literature on rotating credit systems in China, there are many strong statements that participating in rotating credit societies did entail future obligations (Kulp 1925: 191). The need to have a community of people willing to join as members when one needed a large sum of money kept the head or early takers from defaulting: Fei, an ethnographer who worked in China in the 1930s, points out that "Reciprocity is . . . an essential consideration. The defaulter will find it difficult to organize his own society in case of need" (1939: 270). Correspondingly, joining a credit society organized by others in their time of need ensures that they will feel obligated to join yours in your time of need. Emphasis is not on the abstracted sums of interest paid and received, but on the tangible need for a pooled sum of cash. In some cases rotating credit societies were only allowed to serve those needs that did not interfere with community solidarity. Fei makes this clear: marriage or funeral ceremonies were acceptable, "But productive purposes, such as starting a business or buying a piece of land, [were] not so regarded" (1939: 268). In other words, using the accumulated profits to increase stratification within the community was not permitted.

In spite of these ways the credit society could be made to have a leveling function, it is clear it could, if permitted by the community (and this happened in Taiwan and among overseas Chinese), also serve to accumulate more resources in the hands of some than of others, and could lead to capital formation. This supports the idea that these societies were ways in which peasants learned to operate complex financial transactions, deal with profit, interest, credit, and record keeping, and so stood them in good stead to occupy a commercial niche in Southeast Asia (Freedman 1979a).

Even though *hui* have the potential to function like banks, assisting the process of capital accumulation, and splitting communities into richer and poorer, we must not be too fast to assume this was always the case or even the intention. In the uses of *hui* described for Taiwan, for example, these societies function in an environment in which they are strongly disapproved of by the Nationalist state. As an aside here I want to look briefly at the relationship between local accumulations of wealth and the state because it will allow me to make some key comparisons later. The opposition of the state to credit societies is ostensibly because of the risk of default without guarantee (Stites 1982: 269), but probably more realistically it is because of the loss of interest paid to the financial sector, largely dominated by the state (Silin 1976: 23), In this sense, individual Taiwanese may prosper, but in the larger picture, Taiwanese are prospering at the expense of outsiders felt to be collective adversaries.

In Ch'ing China, if peasants had to go outside the community to get credit, they could get locked into exploitative relations with dominant classes: "During the slack season before harvest, . . . labor was abundant but food was often scarce. Hence an extensive, rather complex system of credit was integral to the agrarian economy. This was an important mechanism for tying seemingly independent owner-cultivators to the dominant classes in a dependent relationship" (Stacey 1983: 23). Borrowing money from members of the dominant classes might avoid trouble with other dominant sectors like the state. However, where rotating credit societies could provide the loan, no such dependent relationship need develop.

I have made a similar argument for pigs: that they too were means local populations used to keep resources from the state. Pigs are a kind of precipitate of household productivity, as gold is of exchange, because they turn garbage into valuable pork. In Taiwan there are festivals involving the raising of enormous pigs, called "Honorable Pigs," that are elaborately decorated (Figure 32), offered to the gods (Figure 33) by large communities, and then locally consumed in feasts. For generations, governments have been arguing that these activities waste valuable resources, and trying various ways to legislate them out of existence. The contest is between the state, which would like pork marketed to provide tax and to keep the price low, and the local community, which would like to put on convivial feasts and invite friends and kin, consuming the pork locally (Ahern 1981). Pork and money kept in circulation or consumed in local systems build defensive links among equals at the expense of exploitative links with dominant classes or institutions.

Figure 32. Decorated "Honorable Pigs" in Taiwan. Photo by the author.

Figure 33. Display of "Honorable Pigs" in Taiwan. Photo by the author.

Turning from this aside about the state to other aspects of the *hui*, we can see ways which they are not so much profit-generating devices as devices to translate from one sphere of exchange (cash) to another (commodities that people could produce directly). For example, in one kind of society the head collects, say, $5 from ten associates for a total of $50. "Perhaps a few weeks or a month later, he invites them all to a feast, which costs him about five dollars. This is his first repayment on the installment plan. The organizer does not pay back in cash but in the feasts which he provides at a cost equal to the amount paid to him by each member" (Kulp 1925: 190–91). The author of this account attempts to calculate the profit and loss involved in these exchanges, but I am not sure it is appropriate. What is happening is that small amounts of cash are pooled for the use of each member in turn. But in addition the head is able to exchange $50 worth of rice, vegetables, and meat for the $50 cash. In a village where most of these items could be grown in the course of normal subsistence activities, this amounts to converting the use value of food into the exchange value of cash.

The significance of the transition from goods to money is that certain things could not be obtained without cash. Dealing with government officials and market purchases usually required cash; weddings necessarily entailed the presentation of cash in the engagement fee. Rent in Taiwan is usually paid in cash, and in the Ch'ing, although most rents were paid in kind (grain), a minority of rents in all areas had to be paid in money (Perkins 1969: 105). Since most of these needs for cash only arose from time to time, circulating through the community, rotating credit societies were extremely well suited to handle them.

The central question I am trying to get at is: how did people think of the money that circulated and accumulated in these credit societies? Let me begin to look directly at the imagery and language in which people spoke of these groups. First there is the question whether ordinary participants understood the mechanism of rotating credit societies. Sometimes it is the foreign observers who have the problem: as one put it, rotating credit societies seem "confusion worst confounded, and the maze appears too intricate to the European observer, as he sees in his mind's eye each member transformed, after the first month, one by one, from a lender into a receiver, a borrower, and a payer-back" (Ball 1925: 598). It is precisely because the invariant dominant–subordinate relations we associate with borrowing and lending are absent here that foreigners have difficulty grasping the mechanism. But rural Taiwanese I knew could explain it in a moment.

By far the most complex use of *hui* described in the literature is the New Guinea Chinese system, and its participants seem to have a simple mnemonic for expressing the different positions they can have in different *hui*: *hui* are said to be made up of a "head" and members, known as "legs." "A *Hui* 'leg' who has yet to draw his fund is considered to have a 'living *hui*'" whereas the 'leg' who has already drawn it is said to have a 'dead *hui*.'"The object of joining many *hui* is "always to keep a 'living *hui*'" and a 'dead *hui*' so that a businessman can maintain the necessary capital, absorbing interest from the yet needed living *hui* as a way of saving and maintaining one's reputation" (David Y. H. Wu 1974: 574, 581).

This use of a metaphor comparing *hui* to a living organism—with head and legs, living or dead—is a clue for where to look next. Organic metaphors to describe credit societies abound: Doolittle gives us the "snake-casting-its-skin club," which applies to a club in which members pay the head equal amounts at one time and receive back their portions in turn at stated intervals, "just, as it is said, the snake sheds or casts its skin gradually, or at regulated intervals" (1865, II: 150). Then there is the "Dragon-headed club," in which first payments are larger than later ones, just as the dragon's head is larger than its body (1865, II: 150).

In general, organic metaphors were commonly used to describe economic relationships in China. The basic occupational categorization that ranked agriculture over commerce is explained in the Classics as the difference between the "root" occupation—agriculture—and the "branch" occupation—trade (Kuhn 1984: 20). A Ch'ing writer uses the metaphors of flowers and grass to describe the difference between wealth and poverty:

Wealth and high status are like flowers. They wither in less than a day. Poverty and low status are like grass: they remain green through winter and summer. But when frost and snow ensue, flowers and grass all wither, and when spring breezes suddenly arrive, flowers and grass flourish. Wealth, high status, poverty, low status; being born and being extinguished; rising and declining: this is a principle of heaven and earth. (Quoted in Kuhn 1984: 25)

The significance of these metaphors from natural processes will become clear only when we have looked at how peasants described usury. It goes without saying that interest rates from a landlord or money lender were far higher than the rates prevailing within credit associations (Yang 1952: 97; Tawney 1966: 62; Young 1974: 113). In his famous study of Kaihsienkung, Fei describes how a peasant, desperate to get money to pay his land tax and avoid prison, might borrow from a professional money lender. The amount was set in terms of mulberry leaves, a main crop in this silk-producing area. Money was lent when there were no leaves, and so the rate was set arbitrarily at, say, 70¢ a picul (133 pounds). It was collected when due at the market price of leaves at that time, say $3.00 a picul. Peasants called this "living money of mulberry leaves" (Fei 1939:276). If the debtor could not pay, he might "change to rice," hoping to be able to pay when the rice crop came in. If not, he had to hand over the title to his land. Collection was enforced by violence, or direct reprisals, such as taking a child for sale into slavery. The ultimate recourse of the debtor was to commit suicide at the door of the money lender, which would set his revengeful ghost upon the man, a sanction that was "to a certain extent effective in preventing the usurer from going too far" (1939: 279). It is no wonder the villagers called their money lender "Skin tearer."

In other parts of China similar practices of gross profiting by lending money or grain at an extremely high rate of return were called "cultivating grain flowers" when grain was lent and "cultivating sugar flowers" when sugar was lent (Leonard T. K. Wu 1936: 64, 68). Note that although organic metaphors were used for these forms of usury, much as they were for rotating credit societies, the processes spoken of in usury do not exist in nature! Neither grain nor sugar bears flowers, nor do mulberry trees bear living money. In contrast, the metaphors that describe credit societies belong to common organically related parts of bodies such as a head and legs, or a snake and its skin.

The significance this would have for Chinese is of course not that a natural "law" had been broken. Rather, these events, if they occurred, might well be taken as evidence of a sign from Heaven to high officials that all was not well in the empire. As Joseph Needham says, "The Chinese were not so presumptuous as to suppose that they knew the laws laid down by God for non-human things. . . . The Chinese reaction would undoubtedly have been to treat . . . rare and frightening phenomena as *chhien kao* (reprimands from heaven), and it was the emperor or the provincial governor whose position would have been endangered" (Needham 1956, II: 575). Thus we see there may possibly have been a rebellious connotation to peasants comparing usury to the sort of thing that might be read as a "reprimand from Heaven." Marx noted that capitalists see the interest-bearing aspect of money as its natural property, "much as it is an attribute of pear trees to bear pears" (1967, III: 392). In China pear trees bearing pears would also be seen as a natural property of the tree. But grain-bearing flowers would be taken as a sign that something was awry in the cosmos.

Let us return to New Years debt settlements, which began this lecture. Doolittle describes the dire consequences of failing to settle one's debts to village shopkeepers: "Instances occur when debtors, in despair of being able to pay their debts at the close of the year, and being too proud to bear the disgrace and other consequences of a failure to do so, commit suicide" (1865, II: 86–87). One might wonder if defaulters in a rotating credit society could be brought to the same pass, and indeed they can. David Wu describes a suicide following a spectacular collapse (1974: 581). Others describe somewhat less dire consequences: in Hong Kong if one is in arrears for a long time and does not make contributions by the time the credit society's term is up, one is considered *laan* or "washed up," "rotten" (the same word is used for spoiled fruit), and will not be able to join any credit society in the future. The debtor "may or may not feel he must leave town. In any case, the judgment against him is unreserved and final" (Young 1974: 111). These suicide cases—from default on a debt to a shopkeeper or from default on a credit society debt—result when, so speak, fruit rots, or in other words, someone fails to carry out the forms of everyday sociality expected in local communities. The relationship between the credit society members can be represented by an ordinary thing like fruit, and like fruit, if a member defaults, he will be thrown away.

Encapsulated within these two types of suicides are the two aspects of money we have discussed: a person who cannot meet debts to village shops by New Years or who defaults on a rotating credit society shows his failure to carry on the social trust embodied in money, the trust that the money will travel ceaselessly between people and so help make up the multiple roads of contact that society is comprised of. Losing your reputation means losing others' willingness to include you in these activities, and insofar as your personhood is made up of membership in these groups, if you fail in your obligations to them, you really do cease to exist.

In great contrast is the suicide following the rapacious money lender's seizure of property, described by Fei. This is the face of money that is capable of infinite accumulation at the expense of others. This, expressed as a reprimand from Heaven—flowering grain or money-bearing leaves— is condemned by the revengeful spirit of the debtor's hungry ghost.

Speaking of Southeast Asia and other Asian societies, Clifford Geertz argued that rotating credit societies could run the gamut from an institution with "diffusely social motivations, attitudes, and values as controlling elements" to one with "explicitly economic aims and modes of operation." In my view the whole point about Chinese credit associations is that they bound together in one institution the two faces of money, its social interaction aspect and its individuation aspect. Even in cases where the individuating aspect became a lever by which some could ultimately profit more, as long as people participated in these groups, they were bound by many social considerations. There is no discrimination between "economic" and "non-economic" problems and processes and acting "differentially with respect to them" (Geertz 1962: 261) because both were caught up in the same orbit, bound together in the same institution. Perhaps only when the economic and noneconomic are separated can grain flower and mulberry trees bear money.

I began this lecture with ways China was not a capitalist system before the end of the last dynasty. I have spent most of my time showing how contemporary Taiwan is not a fully blown capitalist society either, because of a variety of local institutions that hold the operation of money and markets within strict bounds. (Next time we will see how in other respects people struggle against the state to increase the operation of markets.) Before ending, I would do well to mention that the PRC has no intention of replicating a full capitalist system either, even though Deng Xiaoping was voted by *Success Magazine* as 1985's "outstanding achiever" (Salisbury 1989: 286).

Despite the glee with which Americans are greeting the opening up of China as a market for American goods (Farnsworth 1986), it is clear China's current leaders are accepting only a limited amount from the market economy. In recent years neither labor nor natural resources are being treated as commodities, planning is still central, although somewhat more flexible, and the ideals of socialism still "constitute the yardstick by which the long-term efficacy of the market mechanism is to be measured" (Hsu 1985: 455). As evidence, the state has acted to enforce injunctions against price-cutting because it might hurt a fellow firm, and to prevent firms from withholding technical information from others (1985: 448).

We may or may not admire these efforts to keep firms from hurting one another, but we can at least see them as similar to the other cases we have discussed. In China today, the state is forcing social issues to predominate over economic gain for individual firms. In nineteenth-century China and Taiwan, social and economic issues were often inextricably bound together by the concepts of shared substance and shared property, the connection between marriage and exchange, and community governance of rotating credit societies. In all these contexts, which I have chosen to emphasize at the expense of others such as usury, taxation, and rent, Morgan's "passion for property" was simply not permitted to become a "commanding force in the human mind."

Although I have said almost nothing about the United States today, I have not forgotten that my four lectures are meant to form a set, the purpose of which is to construct a comparison with our own society. Next time we will look at the meaning of Chinese ritual offerings of money to the gods and at further glosses of theirs on the risks they see involved in capitalist processes. By the end of that lecture, we will be ready to look at the meanings in our own society: of money, imaginary money, gold, and pigs; personhood, value, suicide, and murder; our metaphors of money's magical ability to increase, of how capital grows, and both gustatory and bellicose metaphors of how firms begin, develop, and end.

All this is the better to understand the dense meanings deposited in money, which in Western history have a particularly dark and sinister aspect. For example, there is Chaucer's and Dickens' juxtaposition between money and excrement: Chaucer focusing on an "overweening desire for money which lands most people in the filth of hell" (quoted in Sedgewick 1985: 164); and Dickens on "organic corruption which lay festering in the values that money set, the awful offal of Victorian standards" (Davis, quoted in Sedgewick 1985: 163). And Edgar Allen Poe's juxtaposition between money and the horror of death in "The Gold Bug," of which it is said, "I never saw anything like it before—unless it was a skull, or a death's head—which it more nearly resembles than anything else that has come under my observation" (1889: 13). (No friendly Chinese bones glowing softly in their pots here!) And finally Shakespeare's juxtaposition between usury and consumption, even cannibalism, in *The Merchant of Venice*, where Shylock describes his bargain thus:

> Let the forfeit
> Be nominated for an equal pound
> Of your fair flesh, to be cut off and taken
> In what part of your body pleaseth me.
> (Act 1, Scene 3)

One of my main questions in the next three lectures will be: what happened in the development of Western civilization to set loose the side of money connected with evil and destructive forces at the expense of the side of money connected to sociability and the many roads of human exchange?

CHAPTER II

Spirits and currency in China

The goal of these first two lectures is to see how ordinary people, people subject to oppressive state or economic structures, look at their world, to see what ideas people outside the central institutions of power and control have about the institutions that control them. In some contexts, it is surely true that the "ideas of the ruling class are the ruling ideas" (Marx and Engels 1970: 64). Sometimes people do internalize ideas that serve the purposes of their rulers. Many have elaborated the ways in which the content of ideologies, as well as the educational, artistic, and political institutions that produce them, are in the control of the few at the top, not the many at the bottom (Therborn 1980; Williams 1981). Lewis Henry Morgan himself thought that "capital can rest when labor must be busy; it can contrive when labor is much too occupied to think" (Resek 1960: 53). But I do not believe the story ends here. Those who hear these ideologies, produced by the powerful in the quiet of their mental labors, find ways, amidst the din of their manual labors, to construct their own stories, and organize their own activities.

Last time, I looked at Chinese peasants' and rural workers' concepts of shared substance, shared property, and income, their representations of profit and usury, their valuation of marriage and its relationship to the exchange of money and goods. I argued that in all these contexts, the two contrasting faces of money—its ability to make transactions denser, on the one hand, and its ability to act as a node of personal freedom, on the other—were held together within the same institutions. This is part of why, I think, in late traditional China but continuing into the modern PRC and present-day Taiwan, social considerations govern marriage, labor, property ownership, and credit arrangements and take precedence over the strictly economic ones more characteristic of developed capitalism, such as accumulation for accumulation's sake.

Today I am not going to look further at the movement of money and other commodities around communities per se. Instead I am going to look at ways people represented money, commodities, and the prospect of developing capitalism symbolically, (or indirectly) in ritual. I have three cases that I think serve best: spirit money offered to ancestors and gods; a strange transformation in the character of gods that occurred in north China; and domestic architecture.

In Chinese practice, the living are responsible for the care of their dead relatives in the afterlife, in several different contexts. One context is the underworld, located in some sense physically below this world. Most people say one of the souls of the dead travels to the underworld after death, passing through wild mountainous terrain and narrowly escaping liminal monsters along the way. Once there the soul is subject to judgment for deeds and misdeeds in life before a court like this one, fashioned exactly on the model of the earthly imperial bureaucracy, the magistrate pictured behind his desk meting out punishments to those below. This judgment can be influenced by written petitions for pardon sent by relatives in the world of the living. Eventually, the soul takes up residence in the underworld, living in a house and carrying on the same activities s/he did while alive, until some indefinite time when s/he is reincarnated into another life back on earth.

The living who have recently deceased kinsmen in the underworld try to see that the dead are provided with food, clothing, and shelter or the wherewithal to get it themselves. This is accomplished in two ways: by conveying currency which the dead can use to buy the things and services they need in the underworld or by conveying the objects themselves—houses, clothing, and so on. The currency is made of paper; the objects are constructed of paper and bamboo: all are transferred to the underworld by burning.

The currency includes ritual coins made of silver paper, as well as several kinds of money that are exclusively for the dead in the underworld.

The objects range from sheets of paper stamped with the outlines of clothing or household utensils, through paper replicas of rolls of cloth, to extremely elaborate miniature households. Consider this mid-nineteenth-century description of a "splendid paper house" (Figure 34 shows a Hong Kong version),

Figure 34. Paper spirit house from twentieth-century Hong Kong.

It was some four feet wide in front, extended about three feet back and displayed all the characteristics of Chinese architecture. The interior was furnished after the taste of these people, in the most approved style. In one apartment was a paper dish, out of which a paper pig and a paper fowl were feeding. In another apartment was a paper servant sweeping, and other paper servants were carrying various things about in paper baskets swung on the ends of poles laid across their shoulders. Away in the back part of the house was a paper shrine, with its paper gods and other appurtenances. The whole structure was elevated about two feet above the ground, and presented a very rich and gaudy display. (Anonymous 1849: 372)

Eventually the entire paper mansion would be burned up to send it to the underworld.

Other sources from the nineteenth century describe paper and bamboo horses, sedan chairs, bedding, opium pipes, rugs, spectacles, and furniture (Doolittle 1865, I: 193; Dore 1966: 128; De Groot 1967, II: 717). Ironically, one popular nineteenth-century item was a replica of a fireproof safe, which would be burned up like the rest. In a modern set-up I saw in 1970, a paper house was constructed in a square around a central court. Arrayed inside the court were: two figures of doormen, an electric fan, two television sets, an electric rice pot, a washing machine, a Cadillac, a radio, a refrigerator, and several paper figures of servants wielding mops and brooms.

In part, the hope of the living is that these gifts will prevent the dead from suffering destitution in the underworld, but in part they are also intended to permit them a better life than they were able to have on earth. Consequently, paper houses are often modeled on the houses of officials, or wealthy merchants. One rationale is that "the departed will be treated more courteously and leniently by the constables and judges in Hades if he appears there as a rich man with many possessions" (Fielde 1887: 55). But another, which I heard commonly in Taiwan, is simply that "We try to give the dead the means of living the most comfortable life we can." Hence, the houses are decorated with replicas of aesthetically pleasing gold and ceramic ornaments, and include the most sought-after appliances and vehicles, as well as the prerogatives of wealth: servants and door guards.

When I first saw these paper objects in the field, I initially made the assumption that they should be described as "symbolic," representing the real things they replicate. J. J. M. De Groot, a nineteenth-century sinologist, proceeded along this line, constructing a historical account which sees the paper objects as substitutions, "counterfeits" of real things. Whereas in earlier eras, real objects were burned for the dead or buried with them, by the Han dynasty (second century BC–second century AD), cheaper substitutions began to be made, constructed of clay or wood. Houses small or large and complete with accoutrements like animals and servants were buried in Han tombs. The paper objects used in the present day, which are largely adopted for economic reasons, are seen in this view as survivals of the real things once used (De Groot 1967, I:

706). But even if a case could be made that the present custom of burning paper objects has replaced the original custom of burning or burying real objects, we would still be left with the question why any objects, real or counterfeit, are given to the dead.

A possible answer to this question is that people do not literally intend the dead to benefit by these gifts; rather, they intend them as expressions of wishes or hopes toward the deceased: that they be comfortable in the afterlife and live in the same fashion as the wealthy and powerful. Yet even the meager published accounts of these practices point to a different interpretation. De Groot says,

> It would be a great mistake to suppose that sending mock articles of paper to the next world through the agency of flames was ever considered in China as only an expression of the good will of the survivors to enrich the dead on yonder side of the grave. Numerous exhortations, addressed to the people in sundry books, never to neglect such sacrifices because they really do enrich the dead, point unmistakably to the contrary. (1967, I: 719)

Beyond this, Adele Fielde gives us a hint about what the mechanism is believed to be by which the dead are actually benefited. "These things are supposed to be transmuted, in burning, into the articles which they represent, and to enhance the comfort and wealth of the spirit to whom they are offered" (1887: 55).

Let us look at how my Taiwan informants explained why they offered paper objects, beginning with paper money. The most frequent explanation I was given is that paper things are the currency of the underworld. One farmer said that just as America and Taiwan have different money, so do this world and the underworld, the *yang* world and the *yin* world. He pointed out that when one travels from one country to another, one must go to the bank and exchange one currency for another. In the same way, he said, when one wants to provide things for the ancestors in the underworld, one must make sure to exchange the money and goods we use for those that can be transferred and used in the underworld. In other words, spirit money is just as real as our money; it is just that one must choose the appropriate medium of exchange for the country one is in.

Although they are not money per se, paper replicas of houses and other objects can also be seen as money-like tokens. I had many conversations with a craftsman in a market town, a man in his fifties who constructed paper houses and their furnishings for a living. On the one hand, I asked him whether a very rich man who really wanted to serve his ancestors well could buy actual objects and houses and burn them for his ancestors. The paper house maker said, "No one would do this no matter how rich he was. The real things simply wouldn't burn. A television, for example, is full of wires and all sorts of metal parts. There is no way it could be completely burned."

On the other hand, pursuing my inquiry in what I now see was a doggedly literal way, I asked him whether what arrives in the underworld is a house made of paper, or one made of the usual materials. He replied, "The things that arrive in the underworld are made of real materials. If we make paper bricks on the roof or paper stucco on the walls, the underworld house has a brick roof and stucco walls. The things used in the underworld are also the same size as their equivalents here: they turn into something bigger."Still pressing on, I asked whether the underworld house would have details of construction that were not actually present in the paper house, such things as water pipes, electric wires, and so on. He replied, and would not elaborate further, that the house in the underworld has these things: "They just naturally appear in the finished house." Another villager extrapolated: "The houses and other things are made to show what you see when you look at these things. It doesn't matter that paper is used instead of bricks and plaster as long as the paper looks like the real thing, and since you can't see wires and pipes inside the walls of real houses, they don't have to be in the paper house."These objects are something like Peircian icons, three-dimensional blueprints. The craftsman closed the link to money: "Just as ritual paper money becomes legal tender in the underworld though it is useless here, so paper houses become appropriate for living in the underworld though they would be useless here."

Sometimes money for the dead is made to look as closely as possible like money for the living. Shops in Taiwan that cater to immigrants from Hong Kong sell boxes of coins made of cardboard painted gold or silver and tiny imitations of silver ingots made of silver paper. Nineteenth-century accounts for China refer to mock money for the dead representing "[silver], gold, dollars and cash" (Doolittle 1865, I: 193). In some cases a completely unique form of currency is devised. Taiwanese often burn a form of money for the dead—usually for the amorphous category of ghosts rather than for remembered ancestors—that looks somewhat like American dollar bills. On one side is a picture of an airplane with the inscription "fifty dollars" in English words and Arabic numerals, and on the other side is an oval drawing that appears to be a city of skyscrapers, titled "heaven." Since, as we saw above, people believe that the underworld is, like America, a foreign country that uses different currency, they find foreign-looking money (lettered mostly in English) to be appropriate.

The currency of the world of the living and the currency of the world of the dead are interrelated: I was told that people have to be careful not to give too much money to the *yin* world because it would deplete the stores in the *yang* world. I am not sure I entirely understand the link between *yin* and *yang* stores of money, but one aspect of the link lies in how the values of the two currencies are figured. People said gold and silver spirit money is very cheap to buy—you can get all you need for most occasions with the loose change in your pocket. But paper houses are very expensive, costing several months' income at least. This difference, people said, is because spirit money is simple to manufacture (most of the labor is done as a cottage industry by poor women) (Doolittle 1865, II: 276–77), while paper houses have to be made by a specialist and take several months to complete.

Perhaps one way that sending too many spirit commodities would deplete the money stores of the living is simply that it would use up people's store of cash. Families often have to save for several months or years (or join a rotating credit society) to accumulate enough to pay for a paper house for someone who has died. By the time they purchase it, other relatives have often died and joined the first in waiting for somewhere to live. In such a case, several paper figures representing all the needy ancestors are made and burned, with a deed, at the same time as the paper house. The interdependence and the exchange of one currency for the other can be seen quite literally when Taiwanese "visit the underworld" by traveling there in trance or by listening to reports of others in trance. Often the traveler, whose soul is said to wander about the underworld while s/he is in trance, meets up with someone s/he knows and tries to carry on a conversation. Sometimes, either because the traveler can see that the dead is in need of clothing or money, or because the dead asks specifically for it, the traveler instructs that paper money be burned. Then, those standing by (not in trance) ask anxiously whether it has arrived, and the traveler eventually says yes, the money has materialized in the *yin* world. Sometimes the exchanges go the other way. I was told a story in Taiwan of a hairdresser who washed and set the hair of a female customer late at night. She told him she was to be married the next day. In the morning he heard there was to be a "ghost marriage" (in which the souls of two people who died before marriage are brought together in a wedding ceremony) in the next town. Thereupon he pulled out of his pocket the money his night-time customer had given him and found that it was in fact ritual paper money for the dead.

Just as Chinese currency would be useless in the United States, so ritual money was useless to the hairdresser. This fact is reciprocal: even if Chinese money for the living could be transferred to the dead, numerous people made it clear to me that the money would not be of any use because it would not be legal tender. Spirit money is not so much "counterfeit" as a form of currency one can transform into another currency through burning, on analogy with exchanging one currency for another at a bank.

For the case of modern Taiwan, it makes sense that people should offer the analogy between different currencies themselves because of the exposure all segments of the population have to foreign countries, through television, movies, and employment at subsidiaries of foreign companies. However, one is left wondering what comparable understanding of the function of different currencies peasants in mainland China in centuries past could have had in eras or places where foreign currency was not prevalent. The answer, I suspect, lies within the operation of Chinese currency itself. With regard to copper coinage, we know that there was extensive local variation in the acceptable number of copper coins on a string and in the standard of payment (Lee 1926: 9–11; King 1965: 65).

With respect to silver, the number of different standards of payment was extraordinarily high. Silver was measured by weight and fineness, but there were many different standards, called *taels*. In one town, Chungking, in west China, the standard weight for silver transactions was 555.6 grains. But this was a strictly local value.

> Frequently, . . . a modification of the scale is provided for, depending in some cases upon the places from which the merchant comes or with

which he trades, and in others upon the goods in which he deals. A merchant coming from Kweichow, or trading with that place, will probably, but not certainly, use a scale on which the tael weighs 548.9 grains; a merchant from Kweifu, a town on the Yangtze . . . will buy and sell with a tael of 562.7 grains; and between these two extremes are at least 10 topical weights of tael, all "current" at Chungking. . . . This seems confusion, but we are not yet at the end. Up to this point we have dealt only with the weight on the scale, but now comes in the question of the fineness of the silver with which payment is made. At Chungking three qualities of silver are in common use: "fine silver", "old silver", and "trade silver", and payment may be stipulated in any of these three qualities. Taking the score of current tael weights in combination with the three grades of silver, we have at least 60 currencies possible in this one town. (Morse 1913: 145–46)

Even worse, in the eyes of the foreign observer,

Every little district has its own scale, and every shop in that district differs just a trifle from other shops in reading the scale. If one weighs out 10 taels of silver at home and then goes to a cash shop to turn it into cash, he will find that he has 9.98 taels in one shop, 9.97 taels in another, and perhaps 9.99 taels in another, but never quite 10 taels. (Spalding, quoted in Lee 1926: 14)

However bizarre Westerners found this, only foreigners considered the multiplicity of measures to be a problem in itself:

These chaotic eccentricities would drive any occidental nation to madness in a single generation. . . . Under these grave disabilities the wonder is that the Chinese are able to do any business at all; and yet, as we daily perceive, they are so accustomed to these annoyances, that their burden appears scarcely felt, and the only serious complaint on this score comes from the foreigners. (Wagel, quoted in Lee 1926: 10)

A more tolerant Western observer sums up:

In China you must prove your axioms. We are accustomed to currencies in which the unit of value is a defined and accurate weight of an alloy of

a precious metal . . . of an exact and known degree of fineness. In China
the silver currency is an article of barter, of which neither the weight nor
the quality is anywhere fixed. (Morse 1913: 146)

With regard to paper money, or bank notes, the area within which
they passed as tender was even more circumscribed: they "rarely passed
current beyond the immediate trading area of the town in which they
were issued, and some, issued by merchants, might pass current only
in a particular street" (King 1965: 105; see also Yang 1952: 69–70). So
ordinary people in late traditional China had to be used to converting
one currency to another, even from one street to the next. Converting
money to spirit money is just another example of the same thing. As for
why burning was the means of exchange, I am not sure. It is of course
preeminently a means of transformation of physical substances into another form. Burning paper obviously alters it from paper to ash. Specu-
latively, I might also suggest that there is some resonance with the use
of fire to change mere metal to "coinage." Furnaces were used to mint
copper coins; passing through this fire, they transmuted from a metal
with use value to a coin with exchange value, a value that was intended
to be held timeless and unchanging by the state (King 1965: 139; Sohn-
Rethel 1983).

Now let us look at the major types of spirit money and compare them
to money for the living. Spirit money is divided into three major categories, each with numerous sub-types. First, the highest category—gold
money—is usually considered too valuable to burn for your ancestors,
and so it is burned for powerful, high gods, such as a market town deity.
Second, silver money is burned for lower, less powerful gods, like the
earth god, as well as for ancestors and unrelated spirits, the ghosts. Although spirit money is made of paper, it is meant to replicate the metals
gold and silver. "Many families prefer to fold each sheet into the shape
of a hollow ingot, a procedure which involves much time and labor, but
which is thought to enhance greatly the value of the offering" (Hunter
1937: 52). Third, representations of copper coins, and objects of daily use,
either stamped schematically on sheets of paper or constructed in three
dimensions, were only burned for dead relatives and ghosts.

These three categories of specie correspond roughly to the three
major spheres of exchange that were dominant in late imperial China.

Local purchases, retail transactions dealing with subsistence matters, were made in copper cash. Remittances to officials for taxation had to be made in silver, and this was the metal in which interregional trade was carried out. Unlike copper, silver was not made into coins; even foreign coins such as the Mexican silver dollar were valued by purity and fineness of metal content (Lee 1926: 13–20). The third sector—gold—was reserved for very large payments and for the removal of wealth from circulation, as in the ceremonial treasures of gold wedding ornaments, gold hat pins for successful examination candidates, or the gold statues of the gods (Seaman 1982: 82, 86).

In dealings with living people these three spheres of exchange were kept separate (cash in the market town shops, silver to the magistrate for tax), as was normally the case with spirit money categories. Whether gold or silver paper was being burned at a shrine was nearly always an important clue to whether the spirit being honored was thought of as a powerful god or a minor ghostly spirit. The status of a spirit could change over time if it demonstrated greater powers, and a common marker of this was that the type of money offered would change from silver to gold (Harrell 1974).

In the realm of the living, conversions from one sphere to another were always highly significant. In the conversion of the cash in which taxes were often assessed, to the silver in which they were paid, lay an opportunity for the costs of administration to be hidden. Since copper was generally more available locally than silver currency, taxpayers were allowed to hand in copper coins in lieu of silver. A conversion rate from copper to silver was established by the highest provincial authority and local magistrates were not permitted to exceed this. "However, the prevailing custom among the magistrates was to insist upon payment in copper coins in lieu of silver" (Ch'u 1962: 135), and to change the rate of exchange in their favor. As Gary Seaman (n.d.) points out,

> Although payment could be made in [copper] cash, the central government insisted upon remission in silver, thus it was possible for the official to speculate on the [copper]/silver exchange rate, in addition to whatever margin could be extracted from the taxpayer. The local official and his runner were in a position to increase or decrease the friction in a very large volume of payments, those involving the government.

In the realm of spirit money, conversions from one sphere to another were also highly significant, but for different reasons. Higher-order spirit money, with large ornate gold patterns on paper, was used to mark temporary increases in people's and the ancestors' status and social worth (see Seaman 1982: 87–88). Ancestors, whose offerings were normally held to the sphere of silver, could be offered gold money on the occasions of a son's birth, a wedding engagement, moving into a new (and fancier) house, or large-scale community celebrations like the slaughter of the Honorable Pigs festival (see Lecture I). They were also offered this money when they moved into a new paper house in the underworld. All these are "*hi-su*, happy occasions where families and communities are growing in wealth, members and social standing" (Ahern and Gates 1981: 402). Whereas local people lost and magistrates gained when taxes were converted from copper to silver, here any friction from the exchange is kept within the same kinship system.

Just as the worth of any kind of currency, especially paper currency without intrinsic worth, depends on the consensus of those who will use it, so does the worth of paper articles for the dead. Perhaps this is the force of what people commonly said in Taiwan: that paper things are burned for the dead because "it is the custom." The paper house maker told me, "This is a very old tradition that began in the T'ang dynasty and has been handed down ever since. We just follow that tradition." It could be that these are simply ways of stressing the necessity for conventional acceptance of the worth of these forms of currency, a necessity that applies to paper money for the living as well.

The notion that the worth of paper spirit money and articles is held in place by public trust and political authority is made explicit in the formulas that are recited by Taoist priests when these things are transformed by burning:

> Heaven knows the renown of money.
> Earth knows the reputation of money.
> From *yang* to *yin* it reaches its destination.
> The bundles and the "hundreds" [different sub-types] are not mixed.
> Transformed to burning hot by the fire.
> Riches—sources—treasures—circulators.
> These four words are equally clear.

These ritual formulas are followed by the customary legal phrase paralleling similar communications sent to earthly officials: "Conforming to the order of Tai shang [highest god] and executed with all urgency" (Hou 1975: 93).

Now that we have seen something of the logic of spirit money, its forms and uses, let us turn to its significance. This will lead us to a better understanding of the culture of commerce, profit, debt, and money in China. In short I think that the significance of this practice of offering spirit money differs radically among different segments of the population. The two segments we have some insight into are the petty bourgeoisie in Taiwan (relatively wealthy shopkeepers, craftspeople, and small-scale industrial producers), on the one hand, and rural families (engaged in a combination of wage labor and farming their own land), on the other.

Let us look first at the petty bourgeoisie described by Hill Gates. She discovered in her fieldwork that her entrepreneurial informants constructed a particular version of why spirit money must be burned for the dead, especially a certain kind called "Treasury money," which was burned inside an envelope, called a "suitcase." When a soul in the underworld seeks rebirth, it must first obtain a body and a fate through which to play out its karmic course.

> To do so, it must contract the mystical debt which encumbers each person throughout life. This debt is a sum advanced as a loan to the spirit waiting for reincarnation by one of a large number of Celestial Treasuries, each with its governing official. Part of the money is used to purchase a body for reincarnation; the rest defrays the cost of the individual's particular lot in life, a matter determined prior to birth. Some, indebted for large sums, will receive wealth, high rank, and other blessings in life, while those given less must live with correspondingly straightened means. (Gates 1987: 268)

During one's life one can strive to reduce the debt through the performance of virtuous acts, prayers, and donations of spirit money to the gods. "But, of course, no one ever completely repays the debt. When a person dies, at his funeral relatives must pay off the account by burning great sums of spirit money, if the spirit is to enter unencumbered into a new and presumably more fortunate incarnation" (1987: 268).

Gates ingeniously relates this practice to the form of enterprise her informants were engaged in, suggesting that in these rituals "we see sketched out . . . Marx's classic distinction 'between the circulation of money as capital, and its circulation as mere money.'" As money circulates and returns bearing interest, it becomes "money that is worth more money, value which is greater than itself. It has acquired the occult ability to add value to itself. It brings forth living offspring or at least lays golden eggs" (Marx, quoted in Gates 1987: 273). Gates asks,

> Are these not the transactions in which Taiwan's gods and humans engage and which conclude in the payment of the debt? For human beings, money is a medium by which they exchange part of the fruits of their life's labor for the most essential of "commodities"—a human body and life fate—both of which when consumed, cease to be. Gods, by contrast, lay out money as interest-bearing capital, with an expectation of receiving more than they originally lent: a series of offerings over the lifetime of the individual in the course of normal religious activity, and a final repayment which is usually supplemented with extra amounts. This money returns to the Celestial Treasury to recirculate and expand itself through further capitalist transactions with human souls. (1987: 273)

Gates' explanation for this conception is as follows: first, in late imperial China and present-day Taiwan, the full operation of capitalist markets was (and is) held severely in check by a powerful state. Studies of industry in Taiwan confirm this: firms struggle to obtain the cash, credit, raw materials, land, imports, and access to exports they perceive themselves as needing to do business (Silin 1976: 18, 23). Second, under these conditions, the Chinese populace saw a capitalist world-view as a counter to the feudal-like bureaucracy enforced by the state. Among the attractions of a capitalist world-view, which Simmel would understand perfectly, were that "it offered a social model of upward mobility based directly on wealth rather than on connection with the state through the highly limited channels of degree- and office- holding" (1978: 3).

Consequently, capitalism has come to have a representation in ritual that has a counter-hegemonic aspect. The operations of money could be extolled on shop doors and in proverbs. And its effects as capital could be spelled out in positive terms in ritual. As these small businesspeople see it, they would be better off if the market governed all sorts of transactions, without the intervention of political or social power: using ritual to show capitalist relations lying at the heart of the transactions between people and gods is a way of saying they should lie at the heart of transactions between common people and authorities.

Ingenious as this account is, there are some elements that raise questions in my mind. Is not the ceaseless round of debt, endlessly owed and never repayable, not a somewhat onerous prospect? And what about the Celestial Treasuries: are they the only source of money to secure reincarnation? In De Groot's account, for example, the soul wishing to reincarnate has to borrow from its fellow spirits in order to pay the heavy ransom demanded by the underworld king. The money sent along when a person dies is for paying back a "host of creditors, who are all anxious to collect the funds necessary for their own release" (De Groot 1967, I: 80). This is a picture of a rotating fund, not unlike a rotating credit society, in which the pooled money is used by each person in turn.

I think this puzzle can be resolved if we turn to the second group I have information about, the small farmers and wage earners I did fieldwork with. In these people's view, the money offered to the underworld king is payment in return for services he rendered when the soul was reincarnated, that is, allowing the soul to pass along the roads and through the gates in the underworld. The amount, figured in strict equivalences (1 bill of treasury money = $10,000 NT), is determined by one's date of birth and its associated astrological correspondences. No one mentioned anything about interest, profit, or even debt, simply payment in return for services rendered in the past. In addition the money has to cover current expenses. Every spirit, underling, or god encountered in the underworld, like their earthly counterparts, expected his fee (his squeeze), and dutiful relatives tried to make sure the deceased had enough to cover these expenses. But this is a model of a tributary state, in which surplus is syphoned off from below and held by the center, not, as with Gates' entrepreneurs, a model of capitalist accumulation.

In a description of funeral custom in Peking in the early twentieth century, the model of the tributary state is represented by paper images. Treasury money is packed into chests made of heavy paper and sealed with paper locks. The chests are presided over by "two paper puppets, and the whole under the custodianship of a 'treasury officer', also fabricated of paper. The bearers of the chests are liberally provided with food and drink. Sheets of mock-money, representing advance wages, are tied around each paper figure" (Hunter 1937: 61).

When people talked about the burning of treasury money, their concern lay with keeping it from being robbed by other people or spirits. It was burned at the very end of the funeral ceremonies in large iron stove pots that were old and broken. All the descendants made a ring around the mound of money and stayed in place until it was completely burned up. If they did not, or if outsiders or affines were allowed to be present, "they could steal our wealth." Patrilineal kin linked hands around the stove pots, emblem of their common labor, now broken in death. The emphasis here was on making sure one's own descendant got the amount he or she needed, not, as in Gates' case, on being sure the amount was more than was originally borrowed. I should note that most people I asked had no specific idea what these items were for beyond believing that they somehow helped the dead. Several people stressed their function as a document of communication with the gods of the underworld, showing me that inside the white cover (symbolic of death) you could see the same yellow imperial papers that were burned to the highest god, and hung (maybe you recall?) about the necks of Honorable Pigs. These yellow papers, though called "money," are really "circulators," memorials to officials on imperial yellow paper.

Some written accounts also seem to stress De Groot's idea of a circulating treasure. While describing the debt interest theory, Hou says it is tending to disappear in our day in Taiwan (1975: 29), and stresses that the financial organization of the underworld treasury is not limited to loaning and receiving fees. "It is also a cash deposit box and it may constitute for everyone a reserve where payments are effected in favor of others. Moreover in case of necessity one can make a special payment to augment the account of those interested" (1975: 99). This is far more an image of a corporate community, sharing wealth in turn according to need and trusting that a return will come as one needs it.

Why would these villagers have such a different view of these processes? Their station in life is certainly different from the petty bourgeoisie Gates describes. When I collected this material, most of these people were farmers, and in addition depended on the wage earnings of one or two young people in factories. Sharp distinctions were made between these farming households and those that had successfully made a living in business enterprises: the small shopkeepers, knitting machine operators, owners of a saw mill, cookie factory, or tea processing-operation all paid homage to the village earth god on the 2nd and 16th of the month, in contrast to farmers, who did so on the 1st and 15th.

Although in these ways everyone was aware of the clear difference in modes of livelihood in the community, everyone was also aware of the difficulty of successfully entering business as a livelihood. Business enterprises were perceived as risky, and were known to fail frequently. My landlord and his brother, while not exactly models of caution, attempted to make a go of manufacturing bricks (four times), cans of foam for fixing flat tires, and counterfeit cosmetics (for which I was asked to proofread the English). Over the years I lived in their house, they also tried repairing clocks, and running a printing shop. All these enterprises eventually failed. Operators of small firms were also clearly aware of the risk they bear that as world market demand changes, they may be forced to bear the cost.

For these Taiwanese farmers, capitalism does not represent any kind of sure improvement on life, and it is consequently regarded ambivalently. Perhaps this is why some people (unlike Gates' shopkeepers) tell proverbs that express ambivalence about money and wealth: "Money brings destruction with it." "The poor are happy, the rich have many cares." "Money is as dirt, benevolence and goodness are worth one thousand *taels* of gold."

I have said, on the one hand, that Gates' petty bourgeoisie embrace capitalism and resent the state's limiting of market forces, and, on the other, that rural farmer-workers express ambivalence to capitalism. This leaves us with the question of how peasants regarded the state. Working from this material on spirit money and objects, we can begin to form the outlines of a hunch. First note it was usually the state's prerogative to coin currency. The exchange value of money was supposed to be held constant by the authority of the state. Traditionally and currently, tampering with currency, counterfeiting it, was (and is) a serious crime and could (and can) be punished by death (Yang 1952: 66). That said, now notice we have here masses of people in local populations making, issuing, selling, and exchanging their *own* currency in the form of spirit money for the gods and ancestors! Was this a kind of parody of state power, tongue-in-cheek mimicry of the authority of the state, or an outright usurping of it?

The burning of spirit money to exchange it for another currency even had its direct analogue in state practice of earlier dynasties. In the Yuan dynasty (thirteenth–fourteenth centuries) it was the responsibility of provincial magistrates to oversee the burning of counterfeit paper money. This was done monthly with considerable ceremony, and with increasingly careful governance because the occasion began to be abused by officials, who would embezzle the counterfeit bills instead of burning them (Franke 1949: 49–51; Yang 1952: 66).

At first I thought the idea local populations were imitating state power by issuing currency was a pretty far-fetched one, partly because the spirit money used in Taiwan looks so dissimilar from state money. But then I came upon an actual piece of spirit money used in Peking in the 1930s, and this money could conceivably be mistaken for state money. It was elaborately engraved, numbered, stamped, and printed on heavy crisp paper, "in imitation of genuine money of [that] present day" (Hunter 1937: 63). So it may be local people were not only registering ambivalence to capitalist uses of money, but also, in the very making, issuing, and burning of that money, usurping forms of power meant to be reserved for the state.

In other times and places in China, there were other languages in which ambivalence to capitalism was expressed. In north China the first decades of the twentieth century were a time of profound civil disorder, civil war, invasion, recurrent famine, and breakdown of political control. Local people believed that the images in gods' temples had been taken over by lower animal spirits called euphemistically "the four great families"—fox, weasel, hedgehog, and snake. The story of how this happened was recorded in great detail by a Chinese ethnographer, Li Wei-tsu.

Although these animals were subordinate to the true gods' power and would flee if an earthly official came into their presence, they still had great powers of their own (Li 1948: 21–22). Known politely as the "the gods of wealth," they could protect families of farmers and make them prosperous (1948: 8). In one case all the ripe melons in a field had been collected. The next day, there were as many ripe melons as the day before. In another, a third threshing of wheat yielded an improbably great amount (1948: 11).

However wondrous these abilities, local people were eloquent about their underside. These evilly disposed animals could absorb one's vigor during sexual intercourse (1948: 4) and stir up quarrels among people. "The wicked animals feel greatly satisfied if they can see the anger of the opponents increase and eagerly wait for a final great clash" (1948: 4–5). Furthermore, they were inconstant:

> If they are satisfied with the offerings they receive, they will keep the house in peaceful and prosperous condition, but if the offerings are somewhat meagre they will bring the family to ruin. The gods of wealth are incapable of producing goods, but they can transport goods from one farm to another. The natives call this "*Hsing i chia, pai i chia*", to make one family prosperous by ruining the other. The prosperity of one family may last for several years before it is bestowed upon another family. The losing family loses much more than it has gained through the grace of an animal's spirit. And the *Ts'ai shen yeh* [i.e. the gods of wealth] are commonly very greedy. Every now and then, they demand the repair of their lodgings and more offerings from the family, If their demands are somewhat neglected, they at once get angry, change their minds and confer their favours upon another house. (1948: 11)

There are a number of aspects of this account that make it sound like a commentary upon the risks and shortcomings of developing capitalism. This was an era when, despite many social disruptions, opportunities for some to increase their income were growing: cash cropping, non-farm income, handicraft industries like a rattan factory or tea business were all aided by the growth of Treaty Ports and expansion of the railroads. But these activities may have been seen as risky to the small entrepreneur, as well as capricious and difficult to control. In a sense, this ideology of the "gods of wealth" is a quite accurate view of the nature of these enterprises in which the social division of wealth is seen holistically: the accumulation of wealth in the hands of some means that it will be taken away from others at the same time; wider participation in the market outside the village means that individual fortunes may differ even within families. Accordingly, the attachment of these spirits is not to a family but to an individual: "the native view is that the *Ts'ai-shen yeh* helps only that member of the family which is predestined to be fortuned" (Li 1948: 10). Here we see a picture, not of corporate pools of rotating wealth and family members sharing a destiny and identity with their family, but of individual nodes of wealth, which come and go capriciously and can only do so at the cost of someone else. In a sense this is capitalism unmasked: nowhere here is the misleading ideology so common in the United States that everyone, from General Motors' corporate executives to assembly-line workers, can prosper at once.

For our final case, let us return to Taiwan. In the previous lecture I argued that in various ways people are able to hold off the full development of capitalist forces within the family and community. The question concerning us today is whether people nonetheless see the possibility of more involvement in capitalist processes as a threat (as north China farmers apparently saw it) or whether they would welcome it (as Gates' petty bourgeoisie apparently would). But I have not yet given more than a hint about how the rural people I worked with viewed the prospect of increased involvement in the market economy, commerce, and capitalist enterprises. For this I turn to what they say about domestic architecture.

In looking at the relationship between a society and its cultural attitudes, on the one hand, and house plans and architecture, on the other, I am following in a path opened by Lewis Henry Morgan. In *Houses and House-Life of the American Aborigines* (1881), he contrasted simple house forms and simple social structures with more complex forms. In the villages where I did fieldwork in Taiwan there were considered to be two types of houses: first, a traditional rural house (*Da-cu* or big house), a rectangular structure with a large ceremonial room in the center and bedrooms stretching to either side. As the family grows, wings may be added to either end, forming the classic U-shaped compound. In contrast is the *Yang-lou*, or foreign-style house, usually associated with towns or marketing centers and built (like a Baltimore row house) so that it shares side walls with its neighbor. While *Da-cu* expand out laterally as families grow, *Yang-lou* expand up.

It is obvious that *Da-cu* are suited to places where there is room to expand laterally and *Yang-lou* to places where lateral expansion is unfeasible or prohibitively expensive. The fact that land values are often at a premium in commercialized urban centers means that *Yang-lou* are characteristically found there. In Taiwan there is a dichotomy between rural areas devoted primarily to agriculture, where *Da-cu* are common, and commercial urban areas, where *Yang-lou* are common. This opposition is a key to understanding an important difference between *Da-cu* and *Yang-lou*: when *Da-cu* are built, they must be carefully oriented to the environment according to the principles of geomancy, known in Taiwan as *Di-li*. Normally a professional geomancer is hired to make sure the house faces in the most propitious direction, given the configuration of shapes in the surrounding landscape, the presence of trees, stones, or bridges, the flow of water, and so on. If the fortunes of the inhabitants are doing poorly, one strategy they may adopt is to alter the shape of the landscape or even change the orientation of the house. In sharp contrast, *Yang-lou* are not oriented according to the principles of *Di-li* when they are built. One house builder said, "It's a bother to build a *Da-cu* because you have to be so careful about the *Di-li*. With *Yang-lou* you do not have to build according to the *Di-li*; *Yang-lou* are built according to the road."

The many people who spoke about this distinction between *Da-cu* and *Yang-lou* seemed to have in mind two paradigms. On the one hand, for a farming household located in a rural, relatively unpopulated area and dependent for its livelihood on its own labor and the workings of rain and sun, the *Da-cu* will be oriented according to geomantic principles, stressing this reliance on the environment. On the other hand, for a household engaged in commerce, located in a densely populated, highly commercialized central place, and dependent for its livelihood on its business judgment and the fluctuations of the market, the *Yang-lou* is oriented not according to geomancy but according to the road, stressing reliance on the man-made environment of market demand. The reason for the stress on roads is immediately apparent: they not only provide the physical means by which customers reach one's door, but are also a primary determinant in whether a commercial area will be able to intensify its commercial activity. The two paradigms are relevant not only in the present: informants were sure to stress that even far back in Taiwan's development *Yang-lou* in towns were built "according to the road."

The different ways the houses of farmers and businessmen relate to *Di-li* implies something about different attitudes to the outside world in each case. It could be that people say *Yang-lou* cannot be oriented or reoriented according to *Di-li* simply because the form of architecture (houses in contiguous rows) makes it difficult to change their alignment with the compass, and the small size of the plots they are built on makes changes in the surrounding environment impractical; but even very small adjustments in alignment or in the immediate surroundings could in theory affect the *Di-li*. Yet people declare that bad *Di-li* in a *Yang-lou* cannot be fixed; one can only move out. Hence it seems possible that what people say about the *Di-li* of *Yang-lou* is an indirect way of talking about something else. Perhaps what they are saying is that if one lives in a *Yang-lou*, assuming one engages in commerce, one has a different kind of control over one's fate than if one lives in a *Da-cu*, assuming one engages in farming.

If a farmer's life goes poorly, he can, on the one hand, change the *Di-li* of his *Da-cu* and, on the other, alter his cultivating techniques or plant a different crop. Of course, he might perceive the activity of farming itself to be a failure, sell the land, and switch to another livelihood entirely. But before resorting to that, there would be ample room for changing his methods of dealing with the same raw material, land. Land, after all, can nearly always produce something, especially in Taiwan's generally favorable climate. In contrast, a small industrialist or businessman who found himself without a market for his goods might well have no recourse but to cut his losses and switch to some other line of business. Machinery and raw materials are often more specialized than land: if tatamis (Japanese-style sleeping mats) went out of fashion or the overseas market for sweaters declined, the machines and materials for their production could not readily be put to another use. Like the families in north China with their magical animal families, when the animals fled to another household, they took more with them than the family had earned by their presence. Perhaps this is the parallel in the world of business to the *Yang-lou* whose *Di-li* cannot be altered, but only abandoned. In this connection, it is of the greatest relevance that failure in the small-business sector is very common in Taiwan, partly because of the increasing extent of commercialization and concomitant competition.

What people seem to be saying is that aside from the great potential for wealth and success commerce has, when one abandons a base of agricultural land, one incurs the risk of total failure because one's ability to respond flexibly to changing market conditions is reduced. Or in other words, farmers may be prey to the vagaries of the climate, but over time they can recoup their losses; businessmen are even more prey to the vagaries of the market, and as a consequence may be unable to repair the damage caused by a crisis, just as they are unable to repair the *Di-li* of their houses.

Perhaps the only kind of commercial transaction that is not likely to work this way is one based on spirit money, used as farmers do to pay tribute to powerful officials and to give their ancestors a better life. It may be significant that as religious freedom comes and goes in the People's Republic, so does the open sale of spirit money. I was able to buy ceremonial money fairly openly in Fukien in 1984, and many people were patronizing the nearby temple, where they did not quite dare burn the money, given state opposition to "wasteful superstition," but only set it out as an offering on the altar instead. Spirit money, symbolic in the sense people are relatively in control of what it is believed to "do" in the world, may be the only kind of money people can surely (even in the face of fully sprouted capitalism) prevent from enmeshing them in homogenizing and capricious market forces.

I would like to know how people in China are imbuing the resurgence of spirit money with meaning. Are they eager, incipient entrepreneurs constructing the underworld in the image of a state that (unlike the People's Republic) wholly relishes capitalist relations? Are they, dedicated to socialist principles, returning to old communal forms of rotating wealth that echoed in the land reforms and collectivizations of the thirty years after 1949, but are now being set to one side? Or are they constructing new meanings that reflect on the unique particulars of the present? If we could know, we would have one more way of seeing how this truly "ghostly" spirit money is used by ordinary people to construct their own stories about the forces that bind them.

In the next lecture, I will turn to elements of the second paradox involving money, as I promised earlier: how it causes a socially disintegrating effect by creating feelings of greyness about life as all things come to be measured in the same coin. A final speculation: can it be that one reason money seems not to have done this in China or Taiwan is precisely that money did not operate as a common measure of all things? This claim has been made for economies like the African Tiv, where separate spheres of exchange create incompatible moral values between women, say, and goods (Bohannan 1967). China did not have entirely separate spheres of exchange: conversions could be made, at greater or lesser cost, across the boundaries of the gold, silver, copper, and paper spirit money sectors. But these were surely "bounded sub-systems" (Crump 1981: 131), and they may have served, as people experienced these monies in use, to demarcate different kinds of things: dealings with spirits (through spirit money), dealings with officials and wholesale merchants (through silver), buying objects of daily use (through copper or paper), removing value from exchange (through gold).

Conversions could never be taken for granted because the outcome of them could not be known in advance: conversions were highly particular and specific to different times and places, each with its local configuration of power and politics (Crump 1981: 131). Simmel thought our money would "become the common denominator of all value; . . . hollow out the core of things, their individuality, their specific value, and their incomparability" (1950: 414). But perhaps Chinese money forms, many as they were, served to maintain the incomparability of different things. Instead of the abstract, timeless disembodied value measured by our money, as we will see next time, the value that Chinese money measures is concrete, time-worn, messily embodied, and socially embedded.

CHAPTER III

Money and value in the United States

We now turn to the second paradox I introduced in my first lecture, the paradox that shows how money is inimical to human interaction and potentiality. Remember the two prongs of this paradox: on the one hand there is Simmel's blasé attitude, feelings of greyness about everything. This results from discovering that "honour and conviction, talent and virtue, beauty and salvation of the soul, are exchanged against money," and, as a consequence, "a mocking and frivolous attitude will develop in relation to these higher values that are for sale for the same kind of value as groceries" (1978: 256). On this same hand there is also money's propensity to substitute itself in our thinking for relations among people, because it appears to have a life of its own. In Marx's view this occurs because we think of money as if it were what gives commodities—things produced for sale in the market—their value. In a market economy we do not see the labor that goes into producing commodities, nor do we meet the people who actually produce them. When we go to the grocery store to buy bananas, we do not meet the growers or pickers and so know nothing about the conditions of their lives and labors. To own the bananas, we simply hand over money, and so naturally it seems to us that the money constitutes their value.

The other prong of the paradox is that, instead of producing greyness, confusion, and feelings of moral uncertainty, money can also produce the most intense, clear, and passionately directed feelings toward the accumulation of more of itself, as epitomized by Blaxton's comparison between the usurer and the pig (see Lecture I). As capitalism develops, the ability of money to produce more of itself appears to be an occult power inherent in money, instead of the result of a particular configuration of social relationships (Marx 1967, I: 154–55). Virginia Woolf described this as "the power of my purse to breed ten-shilling notes automatically" (1929: 37).

I will consider how this paradox plays itself out in our society by looking at how the economic sphere and the moral and ethical sphere interpenetrate. Some would find this task a contradiction in terms, for there are many dire statements that here in the final extreme absurdities of late capitalism, the economic sphere has cut loose from any connection with human, moral, or social concerns. Raymond Williams claims, for example, that "the maintenance of the economic system [is] the main factual purpose of all social activities" (1980: 188). But this is an empirical claim, one to which anthropological data could contribute a lot. I will try to suggest what these data might look like—reaching for only the most modest beginnings of a moral economy of capitalism—by first tracing briefly the history of our current setting, and then looking squarely at aspects of how we use money today.

First a brief summary of what I have tried to suggest so far. My first two lectures on China served to establish a contrast between our own economy and another of a very different sort. My goal there was to elucidate with Chinese data Karl Polanyi's finding that for the vast majority of human history, "man's economy [was] submerged in his social relationships. . . . The economic system [was] run on noneconomic motives. . . . The individual's economic interest [was] rarely paramount for the community [kept] all its members from starving" (1944: 46).

Many of Polanyi's insights came from Malinowski's ethnography on the Trobriand Islands—Malinowski was the first anthropologist to observe details of life in a non-Western society first hand—and it is worth looking briefly at one incident Malinowski describes because it throws Polanyi's points into sharp relief, and serves as a transition to societies like our own, where there is a different relation between economy and society. This is the practice some Trobriand communities had of diving for the small mollusk called *lapi*, which formed an important part of their diet. When, upon opening the shell they found "a large, beautifully rounded off pearl, they would throw it to the children to play with" (Malinowski 1965: 19). When European traders discovered this (they were prohibited by the government from organizing diving expeditions themselves), they began efforts to get the islanders to dive for more and more pearls.

The problem the Europeans had was what to offer the Trobrianders as an incentive. The only foreign article Trobrianders desired was tobacco, and their use for it was not infinite. As Malinowski put it, "a native will not value ten cases of trade tobacco as ten times one" (1965: 19). Traders attempted to manufacture native objects of ceremonial wealth—the famous arm shells and necklaces that circulated in *kula* exchange—but the islanders regarded these poor specimens as "dirt." Even when traders found ways of producing acceptable ceremonial valuables, however, they found the islanders could not be induced to dive if there were any community-oriented activities that they had before them. If they had gardening to do, or needed to catch fish to exchange for taro and yams they had received from another community, nothing, as the Europeans saw it, would "make the bloody cows do an honest piece of work on the *lapi*" (1965: 19).

For their part, Trobrianders expressed contempt for the Europeans' "childish acquisitiveness in pearls. . . . Obedience to tradition and the sense of tribal honor make [the Trobriander] invariably put his gardens first, his fishing for exchange second and pearling last of all" (1965: 19). Here truly is a clash between worlds. The islander can smoke some of the tobacco and give the rest away, but his needs for it have limits determined by use. The trader, with access to an economy organized on different principles, can exchange the pearls for money, which he can feel the desire to accumulate infinitely.

However, it would be wrong to suggest that Trobrianders never accumulate things. They may do so, but for entirely different reasons than the traders. As Gregory has put it, "The gift-transactor's motivation is precisely the opposite to the capitalist's: whereas the [capitalist] maximizes net incomings, the [gift-transactor] maximizes net outgoings. The aim of the capitalist is to accumulate profit while the aim of the 'big-man' gift transactor is to acquire a large following of people (gift-debtors) who are obligated to him" (1982: 51). As Firth says of a Polynesian society, chiefs accumulate stocks of certain goods, but they expect to disperse these goods "in a manner which will yield benefit to their people" (1965: 243).

In these kinds of societies, the goods produced have a character that seems strange to us. There is no marked distinction between persons and things (Gregory 1982: 43; Parry 1985). As Leach describes this for the Kachin (Burmese hill people),

> Kachins do not look upon movable property as capital for investment, they regard it rather as an adornment to the person. . . . Wealth objects other than ordinary perishable foodstuffs have value primarily as items of display. The best way to acquire notoriety as the owner (ruler) of an object is publicly to give possession of it to someone else. The recipient, it is true, then has the object, but you retain sovereignty over it since you make yourself the owner (*madu*) of a debt. In sum, the possessor of wealth objects gains merit and prestige mainly through the publicity he achieves in getting rid of them. (1954: 142–43)

This was what Marcel Mauss tried to capture in his book *The Gift*, and what he illustrated by the Maori's notion of the "spirit of the thing given." This spirit, called *hau*, is in a sense part of the person of the original owner, which attaches to a gift he gives. The gift can circulate from owner to owner, but its *hau* always wants to return to its original owner in the form of a return gift. One who fails to return the *hau* might become ill or even die (Mauss 1967: 8–9). Out of a lack of sharp distinctions between persons and things, things come to be thought of as part of persons or as person-like in their own right.

I will now leave this effort to characterize societies in which things relate to people and circulate among them in ways somewhat strange to us, and instead turn to a brief historical sketch of our Western attitudes toward exchange and money, beginning with some antecedents in the medieval period, when debates over the proper uses of money were in full flower. The historian Lester Little has shown how images of money reflected ambivalence when the profit economy began to grow in the eleventh century. By the end of the thirteenth century, the pictorial theme of men or apes defecating coins appeared in the margins of gothic manuscripts; monsters were also depicted vomiting coins (Little

1978: 34). I do not know enough about medieval society to be sure what these images of undigested money might have meant, but it seems possible they were related to the primary view of earlier centuries, St. Thomas Aquinas' original argument against usury. This was that money was a "consumptible in use." For Aquinas, the substance of a good was consumed if its essential form was altered, and money's substance had to be changed in order to use it—that is, it had to be exchanged for something else. Just as wood's substance was altered when exchanged for its heat, so was money's when it was exchanged. This meant that money's use was its substance, its use was its consumption. Usury, then, was not permissible because it entailed selling separately the use of money and the very substance of money. For Aquinas, this was either selling "something that does not exist" (money's substance apart from its use) or selling the same thing twice (Noonan 1957: 54–56). So perhaps the images of vomiting and defecating coins are simply a representation of money not "consumed" in use (not digested), but passed through the body unchanged or arising out of it again unchanged.

However, alongside Aquinas, the thirteenth century saw the first justification for the taking of interest for loans. The new justification for the taking of interest was based on the concept of *damnum emergens* "loss occurring." This meant the lender could justify receiving compensation to return him to the position he would have been in if he had not made the loan (Little 1978: 179). From the middle of the thirteenth century, this became standard practice (1978: 212).

As these ambivalent images suggest, although medieval philosophers were beginning to allow the admissibility of interest, they were far from allowing the uncontrolled taking of interest. Economic interests for them were subordinate to the real business of life, which was salvation. "Economic conduct [was] one aspect of personal conduct, upon which, as on other parts, the rules of morality [were] binding (Tawney 1929: 31). "Economic motives [were] suspect" and so had to be related to a moral end and contained. As St. Antonino put it, "Riches exist for man, not man for riches" (quoted in Tawney 1929: 31).

The emerging concept of interest linked money and time. In spite of this, the dominant view continued to be that "to sell time, which belongs to God, for the advantage of wicked men" was contrary to Scripture and to nature (Tawney 1929: 43). After the commercial revolution of the sixteenth century, further inroads were made on the view that time belonged to God. In Calvinism, credit and the payment of interest were seen as normal and inevitable, and the obligation of seeing that behavior accords with natural justice was thrown on the individual conscience (Tawney 1929: 107; Troeltsch 1956: 643). Nonetheless, early Puritans still held economic behavior within ethical bounds: no interest was to be charged to the needy, buying cheap and selling dear was a vice, and the lender was supposed to share risks with the buyer (Tawney 1929: 215–16; Troeltsch 1956: 644, 648). Some argued that the need of the borrower should determine the interest taken "as his labor, hazard, or poverty doth require" (Tawney 1929: 223). The aim was to subordinate business and enterprise to a "rigorous Christian code of morality that obstructed and confined them" (Samuelsson 1973: 134).

In later Puritanism, where the role of the trader was extolled, social limits to profit were questioned and business enterprise itself became "the discharge of a duty imposed by God." It left the judgment about right conduct in business matters between the individual and his god (Tawney 1929: 230). In Tawney's view, the way was open for our legacy: "a dualism which regards the secular and the religious aspects of life, not as successive stages within a larger unity, but as parallel and independent provinces, governed by different laws, judged by different standards, and amenable to different authorities" (1929: 279).

But this struggle was not over so easily. "Exclusively economic goals were not legitimate in eighteenth-century colonial America, and although this gradually altered over the course of the nineteenth century, mid-nineteenth-century merchants still acted out of social, non-economic roles" (Bender 1978: 112). Lewis Henry Morgan himself instantiated these conflicting tendencies: he was critical of capitalists who measured everything by money but was himself an investor in business enterprises and financed all his studies and political activities on his profits (Resek 1960: 22, 58, 106).

Not until after 1870 did the growth of an autonomous market cause behavior to be unambiguously oriented to the market (Bender 1978: 112). In the late nineteenth century, successful capitalists seemed to feel free to simply divorce moral concerns from economic ones. Thus we have the new view of usury in the words of John D. Rockefeller:

In the early days there was often much discussion as to what should be paid for the use of money. Many people protested that the rate of 10 per cent was outrageous, and none but a wicked man would exact such a charge. I was accustomed to argue that money was worth what it would bring—no one would pay 10 per cent, or 5 per cent, or three per cent, unless the borrower believed that at this rate it was profitable to employ it. . . . All the arguments in the world did not change the rate, and it came down only when the supply of money grew more plentiful. (Quoted in Kirkland 1956: 21–22)

In other words, in his view it is only the market, and nothing about the needs of the borrower, that should determine interest rates.

And again from Rockefeller comes an illustration of how in the late nineteenth century the laws of business were subsumed under the rubrics of natural law and of God's law:

The growth of a large business is merely a survival of the fittest. . . . The American beauty rose can be produced in the splendor and fragrance which bring cheer to its beholder only by sacrificing the early buds which grow up around it. This is not an evil tendency in business. It is merely the working-out of a law of nature and a law of God. (Quoted in Diggins 1978: 13)

In other words, the law of the market is not subject to the law of God, the law of the market *is* the law of God. Even in the face of this enthusiasm, however, there were still critics, as Rockefeller implies, and Lincoln Steffans, Thorstein Veblen, as well as ordinary people in all walks of life, counted among their substantial number (Galambos 1975).

Underlying the translation of the law of the market to the law of God was the fact that both land and labor came to be fully commodities. Workers, lacking access to the means of production, had to sell their labor (part of themselves) as a commodity in return for a wage. Parts of persons were represented as if they were commodities, just as were land, raw materials, whatever. The inextricable connections that we have seen in other societies, between persons and things, humans and land, were broken: things produced, land tilled, could be alienated from the producers and the tillers.

In the late nineteenth and early twentieth century, labor, bodies, time, and space were also increasingly being broken up into segments that could be measured and controlled. The assignment of a monetary worth to a timed segment of a person's labor and the breaking down of that laboring body into machine-like parts according to the principles of scientific management were aspects of the same process (Braverman 1974; Harvey 1985).

In the next lecture I will talk about some living legacies of late-nineteenth-century capitalism. For the rest of the time today, I want to talk in a more general way about the operation of money and value in present US society. The central question is: has the dominance that the economic sphere began to exercise in the late nineteenth century continued? Are there now any limits left at all to the operation of the market? In Morgan's words, does the "idea of property" succeed in dominating "as a passion over all other passions"? (1877: 6). One way to see whether the influence of market forces is all-pervasive is to look for spheres into which our ideology teaches us market forces should reach only lightly—families, face-to-face neighborhoods, small towns, religious groups, and communes. Many have looked, and most have found plenty of limits being set on market forces (Stack 1974; Hostetler 1980). My strategy will be to look straight at the sphere of purchase and spending, banking, investment, and capital formation, as carried out by individuals and institutions, to confront directly what Simmel called the "nurseries of cynicism" (1978: 256). Here, I think, a darker, more contradictory struggle for human dignity goes on.

My tactic will be to look at three different but related processes that have been held to occur in capitalist society, each of which involves the increasing dominion of money or models of money making over all else. In each case I will discuss whether there is resistance and struggle against the take-over. I will look first at capital as the "general illumination" of everything in society, second at money as the "frightful leveler" of everything, and third at the "boundless greed" that can accompany the development of capitalism, where money is passionately sought for its own sake as well as for the sake of the things and power it can buy. With one exception this discussion should be heard as a proposal for fieldwork rather than a report on it. I have gathered what I could as a regular participant in our society, rather as Humphrey Jennings selected what he

called "images," moments in the course of the history of industrialization that seemed to him to illustrate and concentrate complex forces and
struggles (1985: xviii).

First, let us look at the tendency of capitalism to serve as a "general
illumination" of all else. At the end of *Ancient Society*, Morgan reflects
on the consequences of the growth of property in civilization. "The out-
growth of property has been so immense, its forms so diversified, its uses
so expanding and its management so intelligent in the interests of its
owners, that it has become, on the part of the people, an unmanageable
power. The human mind stands bewildered in the presence of its own
creation" (1877: 552). Continuing this thought, Marx said,

> In all forms of society there is a specific kind of production which pre-
> dominates over the rest, whose relations thus assign rank and influence to
> the others. It is a general illumination which bathes all the other colours
> and modifies their particularity. It is a particular ether which determines
> the specific gravity of every being which has materialized with it. . . .
> Capital is the all-dominating power of bourgeois society. (1973: 607)

What can be said empirically about the "general illumination" shed
by the capitalist market on our lives? I think the problem has two aspects: first, the extension of models of capitalist enterprises onto entities
outside them; and, second, the application of market principles to things
formerly outside the marketplace.

I will begin by talking about some aspects of the "general illumination" of the market on other areas of life, which I came upon quite by
accident. In the course of doing research over the last three years on
how women's bodies are represented in scientific language, I discovered
many central metaphors that seemed taken directly from the realm of
production and applied to female reproduction. Let us start with views
of the body that prevailed somewhat earlier in history. It can be shown
that the view of the body as a balanced intake–outgo system shifted
during the nineteenth century to the body as a small business trying to
spend, save, or balance its accounts. Another shift began in the twentieth century with the development of scientific medicine. One of the
early-twentieth-century engineers of our system of scientific medicine,
Frederick T. Gates, who advised John D. Rockefeller on how to use his

philanthropies to aid societal well-being, employed a series of interrelated metaphors to explain the scientific view of how the body works:

> It is interesting to note the striking comparisons between the human body and the safety and hygienic appliances of a great city. Just as in the streets of a great city we have "white angels" posted everywhere to gather up poisonous materials from the streets, so in the great streets and avenues of the body, namely the arteries and the blood vessels, there are brigades of corpuscles, white in color like the "white angels," whose function it is to gather up into sacks, formed by their own bodies, and disinfect or eliminate all poisonous substances found in the blood. The body has a network of insulated nerves, like telephone wires, which transmit instantaneous alarms at every point of danger. The body is furnished with the most elaborate police system, with hundreds of police stations to which the criminal elements are carried by the police and jailed. I refer to the great numbers of sanitary glands, skillfully placed at points where vicious germs find entrance, especially about the mouth and throat. The body has a most complete and elaborate sewer system. There are wonderful laboratories placed at convenient points for a subtle brewing of skillful medicines. . . . The fact is that the human body is made up on an infinite number of microscopic cells. Each one of these cells is a small chemical laboratory, into which its own appropriate raw material is constantly being introduced, the processes of chemical separation and combination are constantly taking place automatically, and its own appropriate finished product being necessary for the life and health of the body. Not only is this so, but the great organs of the body like the liver, stomach, pancreas, kidneys, gall bladder, are great local manufacturing centers, formed of groups of cells in infinite numbers, manufacturing the same sorts of products, just as industries of the same kind are often grouped in specific districts. (Quoted in Berliner 1982: 170–71)

Elements of the images that occurred to Gates are still commonplace. In recent years, the "imagery of the cell [has] been that of the factory." And moving to slightly more complex functions involving money and banking, ATP (a chemical compound produced by cells) is seen as the body's "energy currency": "Produced in particular cellular regions, it [is] placed in an 'energy bank' in which it [is] maintained in two forms, those of 'current account' and 'deposit account'" (Lewontin, Rose, and Kamin, 1984: 59; see also Guyton 1986: 23–24).

Development of the new molecular biology brought additional metaphors based on information science, management, and control. In this model, flow of information between DNA and RNA leads to the production of protein. Molecular biologists conceive of the cell as "an assembly line factory in which the DNA blueprints are interpreted and raw materials fabricated" (Lewontin, Rose, and Kamin 1984: 59). The cell is still seen as a factory, but, compared to Gates, there is enormous elaboration of the flow of information from one "department" of the body to another, and of the exertion of control from the center, the brain.

The view of the body as a hierarchically organized bureaucratic system of control has profound implications for how a basic change in the system is perceived. For women, this occurs most dramatically at menopause, and it is no accident that in medical terms menopause is seen as a failure or breakdown of central control: ovaries become "unresponsive"; the hypothalamus begins to give "inappropriate orders." For lack of time I will not pursue this further here.

Instead, let us return to metaphors we have seen dominate the smallest units of the body, cells, namely the factory producing various substances. At the cellular level, DNA communicates with RNA, all for the purpose of the cell's production of proteins. It would be no surprise, therefore, if the system of communication involving female reproduction were also thought to be geared toward production of various things. It is clear that the system is thought to produce many good things: the ovaries produce estrogen, the pituitary produces FSH and LH, and so on. Beyond all this the system is seen as organized for a single preeminent purpose: "transport" of the egg along its journey from the ovary to the uterus (Vander, Sherman, and Luciano 1980: 503) and preparation of an appropriate place for the egg to grow if it is fertilized.

Yet I would like to suggest that assuming this view of the purpose of the process slants our description and understanding of the female cycle in a particular direction. Let us look at how menstruation is described. First of all, the action of progesterone and estrogen on the lining of the uterus is seen as "ideally suited to provide a hospitable environment for implantation of a fertilized ovum" (Vander, Sherman, and Luciano 1980: 501).

Given this teleological interpretation of what the increased amount of uterine lining is for, it should be no surprise that when a fertilized egg does not implant, the next thing that happens is described in very negative terms. The fall in blood progesterone and estrogen "deprives" the "highly developed endometrial lining of its hormonal support," "constriction" of blood vessels leads to a "diminished" supply of oxygen and nutrients, and finally "disintegration starts, the entire lining begins to slough, and the menstrual flow begins" (Vander, Sherman, and Luciano 1980: 501). Blood vessels in the endometrium "hemorrhage" and the menstrual flow "consists of this blood mixed with endometrial debris" (1980: 501), while the "loss" of hormonal stimulation causes "necrosis" (Guyton 1986: 976).

The construction of these events in terms of a purpose that has failed is beautifully captured in a standard text for medical students—a text otherwise noteworthy for its extremely objective, factual descriptions—in which a discussion of the events covered in the last paragraph (sloughing, hemorrhaging) ends with the statement, "When fertilization fails to occur, the endometrium is shed, and a new cycle starts. This is why it used to be taught that 'menstruation is the uterus crying for lack of a baby'" (Ganog 1983: 356).

I am arguing that just as seeing menopause as a kind of failure of the authority structure in the body contributes to our negative view of it, so does seeing menstruation as failed production contribute to our negative view of it. Sontag (1979) stresses our horror of production out of control. But another kind of horror for us is lack of production: the disused factory, failed business, idle machine. Winner terms the stopping and breakdown of technological systems in modern society "apraxia" (1977: 185), and describes it as "the ultimate horror, a condition to be avoided at all costs" (1977: 187).

Menstruation not only carries with it an overlay of a productive system that has failed to be productive, it also carries the idea of production gone awry, making products of no use, not to specification, unsalable, wasted, scrap. However disgusting it may be, menstrual blood will come out. Production gone awry is also an image that fills us with dismay and horror. Amidst the glorification of machinery common in the nineteenth century were also fears of what machines could do if they went out of control. Consider, for example, the steam-operated shaving machine that "sliced the noses off too many customers" (Fisher 1967: 153), Melville's character, an allegory of America, who was killed by his mechanical slave (Fisher 1966; 1967: 153), as well as Mumford's image of modern machinery as a sorcerer's apprentice (Mumford 1967: 282).

It may be that an element in the negativity attached to imaging menstruation as failure to produce is precisely the view that women are in some terrible sense out of control when they menstruate instead of getting pregnant. They are not reproducing, not continuing the species, not preparing to stay at home with the baby, not providing a safe, warm womb to nurture a man's sperm. Whether or not this suggestion can be supported, I think it is plain that the negative power behind the image of failure to produce can be considerable when applied metaphorically to women's bodies. In a description of menstruation in one standard text, one is confronted in rapid succession with "degenerate," "decline," "withdrawn," "spasms," "lack," "weakened," "leak," "deteriorate," "discharge," and, after all that, "repair" (Mason 1983: 525).

In another standard text, we are presented with imagery of catastrophic disintegration: "ceasing," "dying," "losing," "denuding", and "expelling," and the accompanying illustration captures the explosive decomposition exactly (Guyton 1984). You may be thinking, as I did at first, that for all the negative connotations of these images, surely they simply represent what menstruation actually, scientifically is. To see that it is not menstruation's scientific destiny to be described this way, however, consider how medical texts describe men's production of sperm. One example: "The mechanisms which guide the *remarkable* cellular transformation from spermatid to mature sperm remain uncertain. . . . Perhaps the most *amazing* characteristic of spermatogenesis is its *sheer magnitude*: the normal human male may manufacture several hundred million sperm per day" (Vander, Sherman, and Luciano 1980: 483–84, emphases added). It is, in terms of my argument, certainly no accident that this "remarkable" process involves precisely what menstruation does not in the medical view—production of something deemed valuable. Although the texts see this massive sperm production as unabashedly positive, in fact, only about one out of every 100 billion sperm ever makes it to fertilize an egg: from the very same point of view that sees menstruation as a waste product, surely here is something really worth crying about!

Although the image of menstruation as failed production surely exists and, I think, exacts a toll in the medical treatment of women, it is not swallowed uncomplainingly by all women. Interestingly enough, my study showed that working-class women refuse to talk about menstruation in these terms, rejecting the notion that menstruation centrally represents a failure. Instead, their descriptions reflect its phenomenology: how it looks and feels; what it is like to be a woman experiencing the event and what its significance is in her life. In sum, the elements of the operation of capitalism that "bathe" the colors and particularities of men's and women's bodies are the emphasis on relentless production of substances seen as valuable (sperm) and denigration of substances that represent unused "machinery" or failed "production."

A second aspect of the "general illumination" of capitalism is the extension of what we are willing to consider can be bought and sold on the market. Marx saw this process as inevitable but regrettable. He spoke of things that "are in themselves no commodities, such as conscience, honour, &c., being offered for sale by their holders, and of thus acquiring, through their price, the form of commodities. Hence, an object may have a price without value. The price in that case is imaginary, like certain quantities in mathematics" (1967, I: 102). He used the term "imaginary price" to capture the sense he had that these are not the sort of things a price can be put on. Similarly, Winner uses the term "perverse" for this process: "instances in which things have become senselessly or inappropriately efficient, speedy, rationalized, measured, or technically refined. . . . It is not that such norms are perverse in themselves but rather that they have escaped their accustomed sphere" (1977: 230).

Michael Walzer's work comes in here, as he lists all the kinds of "blocked exchanges" he could see in the early 1980s, ways we set limits on the domination of wealth. The things he thought we still today do not believe should be bought and sold include: human beings, political power and influence, criminal justice, freedom of speech, marriage and procreative rights, exemption from military service, political office, prizes and honors, divine grace, and love and friendship (1983: 97–103). Even though individuals may attempt to buy or sell these things, they try to hide what they are doing, and are punished in various ways if they are caught.

The example I will look at a little more closely is the buying and selling of body parts for transplant and the buying and selling of the materials of reproduction. First body parts. In the last few years various direct efforts have been made to profit from the buying and selling of kidneys and other organs. A Virginia doctor set up a business to broker human kidneys. A person who needed the money would sell a kidney to a person who needed it, and the doctor would take a fee for his services (Goodman 1983). Another scheme provided for people to sell or buy organs in an international market (*Washington Post*, September 19, 1983: A9). These developments were met with vigorous opposition by Senator Albert Gore, who attached a provision prohibiting the buying and selling of body parts to a bill—since passed—designed to assist non-profit organ procurement organizations. His reasons are forcefully stated. In his testimony before the subcommittee on health and the environment, he argued that these activities must be prevented "to protect that which is uniquely human." In the press he is quoted as saying, "Our system of values isn't supposed to allow the auctioning off of life to the highest bidder . . . it erodes the distinction between things and people" (Goodman 1983). Instead of the extension of personhood to things that we saw earlier among the Kachin, Maori, and Chinese, here the worry is that thinghood will be extended to persons.

Turning to other parts of the body, it is now acceptable to sell sperm, perhaps because they are a renewable resource, and one that can fairly easily be quality controlled. Many a Hopkins medical student has enjoyed the extra cash from the bonus price he gets from his desirable sperm. But the buying and selling of human eggs (they are already being "harvested") has not yet occurred, despite the commonplace of women selling—"renting?"—their wombs for surrogate motherhood. In the United States this has produced concerned publications from feminists, but no organized federal effort to control it. In England, things stand on a more advanced footing. The Warnock Report, a report of a committee charged to "examine recent, and potential developments in the field of human assisted reproduction," was published in 1984. It found it "inconsistent with human dignity that a woman should use her uterus for profit" (Rivière 1985: 5); and degrading to the child so born, since it will have been bought for money (1985: 5).

We have seen examples of the state stepping in to stop market forces (Senator Gore), and of communities of concerned citizens raising a public outcry (the Warnock Report). At other times the law is a constraining force. There is a fascinating story I have no time to tell of how, beginning in the late nineteenth century, the function of American law changed to encourage and protect market processes (Hurst 1956, 1982). Despite this change, the law continues to hold out some protections against the market exceeding its limits, and this is made plain in recent events concerning a debacle in Baltimore's savings and loan industry. The press and official reports describe a "virtually unregulated industry tainted by the greed and cunning of some savings and loan executives" (LoLordo 1986). Owing to "pervasive self-dealing," these savings and loans were "a burden on the community which [they] supposedly serve[d]" (Report 1986: 150). "It was a way of life . . . a way of life that had built up contrary to law" (Su1lam 1986).

Chief among the villains in the case was Jeffrey Levitt, the president of a local savings and loan association. Charged with buying what was not legally his to buy, selling what was not legally his to sell, and spending over $14.6 million of depositors' funds, he was indicted on twenty-five counts of theft and misappropriation of funds. To understand the cultural sense in which Levitt is understood to have transgressed, we must look at some metaphors of food and eating applied to corporations, appropriate enough since corporations are in fact regarded in the law as persons and might as well have at least metaphorical bodies. These metaphors are particularly common in talk of mergers when we say one company is being gobbled up or swallowed by another. Sometimes this corporate ingestion is neutral and sometimes it is aggressive, as in an ad that showed money owed being gleefully gobbled up by a gremlin-like monster while the debtor goes down the tubes. But the metaphors go far beyond this: real estate deals that buy up unfinished properties at bargain rates are called "vulture funds," and those that fail "end up getting their eyes picked out" (Lipman 1986). A recent device that companies use to avoid being consumed in a take-over bid is called a "poison pill" (Hertzberg 1986). Then there are defense contractors who can "stay fat on the leftovers" or reduced budgets (*Business Week*, January 13, 1986: 63). And for those companies that have eaten too many leftovers, corporate America is "dieting its way to increased efficiency, in part by spinning off money-losing subsidiaries and divisions" (*Money*, January 1986: 83). Some of the food corporations eat is, as one might expect, not healthy. "Junk" bonds, risky, high-yielding IOUs that aid mergers, are spoken of as "the juice that made the party go." But, like a wise parent, the Federal Reserve "is watering down the punch" (*Time*, January 20, 1986).

It is in this context that much has been made in the press of how much Levitt and his wife eat at restaurants: rich meals, many elaborate desserts, some consumed on the spot and others boxed to take home. The Attorney General described Levitt as using "Old Court Savings and Loan as his private trough, at which he fed, a trough which was continually replenished with other people's money" (Frece 1986). A local columnist summed it up: "the massive food-intake is a metaphor for all of the charges against them. While others cannot get to their money, the Levitts have eaten cake" (Olesker 1986). Here we see a corporate "body" embodied in a real-life glutton, stopped in his tracks because he crossed clear limits in the law about what property he owned and therefore what he could buy and sell. Instead of Chinese pigs who transform waste into wealth and capture resources for local communities against the state, we have here something more akin to Blaxton's swinish usurer who spoils good crops and who gives no profit to the community while he lives among it. Pigs are sweet and innocent emblems of accumulation (Sidney W. Mintz 1964: 272) for us as long as they do not become, as Levitt did, wild hogs, in Blaxton's words, "running thorough, and tearing of hedges: eating and devouring up good Corne, Beanes and Peason" (see Lecture I). We have gone from monkeys defecating money to pigs growing fat on it as images of money's harmfulness.

In *Timon of Athens*, Shakespeare says of gold:

> Yellow glittering, precious gold? . . .
> thus much of this will make black, white; foul, fair;
> Wrong, right; base, noble; old, young; coward, valiant,
> . . . Why this
> Will lug your priests and servants from your sides;
> Pluck stout men's pillows from below their heads;
> This yellow slave
> Will knit and break religion; bless th'accurst;
> Make the hoar leprosy adored; place thieves,
> And give them title, knee, and approbation,
> With senators on the bench.
> (Act 4, Scene 3)

This leads us to our second main theme, the moral confusion and uncertainty that surround us in a late capitalist country. Simmel puts it like this:

> The essence of the blasé attitude consists in the blunting of discrimination. This does not mean that the objects are not perceived, but rather that the meaning and differing value of things, and thereby the things themselves, are experienced as insubstantial. They appear to the blasé person in an evenly flat and gray tone; no one object deserves preference over any other. . . . By being the equivalent to all the manifold things in one and the same way, money becomes the most frightful leveler. . . . All things float with equal specific gravity in the constantly moving stream of money. (1950: 414)

I will now look briefly at two cases that illustrate how people struggle with the "frightful leveler." Around the Christmas of 1983, as many of you who are parents of young children will remember, there was an extreme scarcity of a commodity many children desperately wanted: Cabbage Patch dolls. (Since then they have become too plentiful.) A minor scandal was created in the Baltimore area as lucky parents who had bought a doll early, or happened upon a rare shipment being unloaded, decided to forgo the pleasure the doll would give their children for the high price it could bring in the classified ads. (Dolls bought for around $30 were being advertised and sold for several hundred dollars.) One parent explained, in a phrase that tells it all, "money became thicker than blood!" (Henderson 1983). A spokesperson from Coleco, the company that was responsible both for the massive advertising that hurled the dolls into such demand and for the shortage, chastised those who chose to sell: "It's just too bad people out there are willing to take advantage of parents' emotions. Coleco is recommending that parents control their emotions, she said" (Henderson 1983). However, the struggle was not over control, but over measuring disparate things in the same coin. One woman said, "This is all crazy." She had to decide whether to sell the dolls she had bought to please her children or forgo an expensive operation her dog needed: "My husband said shoot the dog or sell the dolls" (Henderson 1983). Money has become so inexorably the means of showing love, even to a dog, that we are forced to set these incommensurable things alongside each other and choose. It is ironic that this doll, itself a commoditization of parenthood, should lead to further exchanges of blood for money. Cabbage Patch dolls come with a birth certificate identifying each unique individual doll by its footprints, and the child is encouraged to send for its adoption papers.

We have looked at money as the "general illuminator" and the "frightful leveler." Let us now look at the tendency of money in capitalism to be associated with infinite accumulation. As Marx explains it,

> This boundless greed after riches, this passionate chase after exchange-value, is common to the capitalist and the miser; but while the miser is merely a capitalist gone mad, the capitalist is a rational miser. The never-ending augmentation of exchange-value, which the miser strives after, by seeking to save his money from circulation, is attained by the more acute capitalist, by constantly throwing it afresh into circulation. (1967, I: 153)

There are two kinds of reasons for this relentless accumulating and spending. The first is that it is in the nature of a competitive free market that enterprises must win or lose, compete successfully or fail. It is no figment of the advertising companies' imagination that companies must grow, undersell, out-produce, create new products, find new markets, or go out of business. With respect to companies trying to market the same thing, when you come in second, you really do lose the race.

The language of business magazines captures the baleful aspects of these struggles in vivid ways. One series of connected metaphors starts out innocently enough. (We have made the acquaintance of a series of gustatory metaphors, now we see barnyard ones.) We all know about nest eggs, but what happens when they hatch? New enterprises are seen as hatched eggs (*Forbes*, December 2, 1985), and twenty-nine states now have "business incubators" that offer advice, space, and secretarial services to "fledgling" entrepreneurs (*Money*, January 1986: 27). When these fledglings try to fly, the imagery abruptly changes, or rather the avian imagery is extended to match the experience of birds in real life: for businesses as for birds, there is no protected adolescence. We hear of a "bloodbath" (*Business Week*, January 13, 1986: 35), a business being "at death's door" (1986: 35), or, somewhat better, "off its deathbed but just limping along" (1986: 72), or "needing only outpatient treatment"

(1986: 72). Then there is "suicidal price cutting" (1986: 35), and finally "falling into the abyss" (1986: 79).

In an atmosphere like this, it is easy to see how companies might act in ways that hurt other people or the environment out of a desire to survive. But what is the "inner logic of the practice" in capitalism that sometimes leads to behavior that hurts other people? Marx was clear that just as precapitalist economic behavior is not produced because people are especially altruistic in character, so capitalist economic behavior is not produced because we have especially many villains among us. How then does it happen that General Motors marketed and aggressively sold the Corvair to young adults (many of them children of GM executives) when it was known the car had serious design faults? How did it happen that A. H. Robins continued to sell the Dalkon shield after it was known to cause infection, death, and sterility, and how could it happen that Robins sold the shield in the third world after they were stopped from selling it in the United States (Dowie 1979; Morton Mintz 1985)?

A part of the answer is that the cut-throat nature of competition focuses attention on the need to increase production and sales to survive. (Even now legislation is pending before Congress to "legalize the export of drugs not yet approved by the FDA [Food and Drug Administration] to 15 industrialized countries provided they license the drugs first" [*Business Week*, January 13, 1986: 92]. The rationale is because it would increase drug exports by $500 million annually.) Another part of the answer goes back to the notion of money taking on a life of its own. Marx argued that the process of money taking on its own life so that it appears to be the value in commodities blinds us to the true value they have (the labor that created them), and blinds us to the conditions of life of those who produced them. I would like to add that when money seems to come alive, it can also blind us to the social effects of throwing commodities into the market in return for money. The money in unsold inventories has a way of rising up and demanding to be reclaimed, at any cost. Just as the conditions of production are concealed within the money form, so are the conditions of selling.

A particularly vivid example of how money seems to be caught like a frozen being inside commodities, from whence it cries out to be released, came in a radio ad for the classified ads in the Baltimore *Sun*. Here is the text of one of the spots:

FORGOTTEN MONEY: Hello. You don't know me. But you sure could use me. I'm your forgotten money: all the cash you put into new things that you just don't use anymore. But you can get me back fast. Just list your unused car . . . piano . . . boat or whatever in the Baltimore *Sun* . . . Do it tomorrow and in just a day or two, I'll be filling your wallet once again.

The vast quantities of Dalkon shields that were sold in the third world had already been manufactured when their harmful effects were discovered. If forgotten money in an old piano cries out plaintively, think what a clamor the money in these huge inventories must have made in the ears of Robins corporate executives.

This is far from the whole story, of course. Every case of corporate action I know of that hurts the public includes tales of individuals in the corporation who object, resist, and even quit. GM employees who knew about the Corvair's design faults tried in many ways to stop it and were threatened with the loss of their jobs (Wright 1979: 66–69). Hugh Davis, the inventor of the Dalkon shield, claims he objected to its continued sale after its problems became known, and in any case, he quit his affiliation with the company. (But see Morton Mintz 1985 for a sorrier version.)

We are looking at aspects of the "boundless greed after riches," where, even in the available material (unfortunately not yet based on fieldwork), there are hints that these events contain struggles over moral issues. I will now turn to a case involving small-scale enterprises to see in more detail some ingredients of these struggles. The case I would like to consider briefly is the relation between farmers and bankers in the Midwest. On December 9, 1986, Dale Burr, a farmer in Iowa, about to lose his land, his machinery, his stored grains, and his beloved quarter horses, is alleged to have killed his wife, his bank president, a neighbor with whom he had quarreled over land, and finally himself. "At 11:22 AM he walked in the back door of the shiny modern bank on Main Street where his checking account was overdrawn. He pulled the long, pump action gun from his overalls and fired one blast at Mr. Hughes's head as the 46 year old bank president looked up from his office chair" (Malcolm 1985a).

Short of murder and suicide, tension between bankers and farmers is widespread: a survey of 155 bankers in Iowa found 45 percent characterized relations with farmers as tense. "Half the bankers said they had been verbally abused, 13% had been physically threatened and 4% were actually attacked" (Malcolm 1985a). Farmers and bankers alike see this "fear and frustration, this stress and sense of powerlessness [coming] from decisions made so far away: interest rates, crop prices, grain embargoes and even foreclosures by government agencies or by the main office of a local bank recently consumed by a merger" (Malcolm 1985b). It is not hard to see how a farmer faced with failure to carry on his family's legacy might take his own life and even those of others he felt were part of his life, or responsible for his failure. In the words of a farmer whose fields lie in the county south of Dale Burr's, on the day after the murder–suicide:

> It's a terrible experience when a farm goes under. You take a farmer who has lived on the farm his whole life—a farm that's been passed on for maybe generations—and suddenly someone is just taking it away, or they're telling him how he has to do his work. It's hard. There's a lot of pressure. . . . If it was a farmer who shot John Hughes and the others, it was probably that he just couldn't handle the pressure any more. It just got to him. (*Iowa City Press-Citizen*, December 10, 1985: A1)

A Georgia woman said of her father, who committed suicide moments before his property was to be auctioned for unpaid debts, "He just couldn't stand to see his whole life go on the steps 'of the courthouse'" (Rehert 1986).

Apart from the sense of failure, another ingredient in these violent events is clearly the breakdown of the hallowed American links among labor, productivity, and reward. In the weeks before the Burr suicide and murder, a local Iowa art teacher created the character Farmbo, a combination of Rambo, the violent Vietnam vet, and Brant Wood's stoic American Gothic Farmer. His purpose was to create a positive comment on fighting back against hard times, the fighting to be done by hard work. The caption reads, "the most productive man in the world—will be back." The trouble is that farmers' experience says loudly that hard work is no longer leading to success and rewards. As one Maryland farmer put it, "It all seems so futile. The harder I work the less I have to show for it"; and another echoes the same words: "It all seems so futile. No matter how hard you work or what record yields you get, you wind up beaten in the end. In 1979 we were getting $6.90 for a bushel of soybeans. Today we're getting $4.70" (Rehert 1986).

Behind this dismay over declining profits is the fear that the land itself will be lost. No matter how much labor and sweat these workers invest in it, as an alienable commodity it can be sold out from under them. Nonetheless, farmers and local political organizations continue to resist this definition of family farm land as a commodity, urging: a moratorium on foreclosures, allowing farmers to 'homestead' on a small portion of the bankrupt farm, giving the farmer the right to repurchase his farm, or to pass this right on to his children (Iowa Farm Unity Coalition 1986; *Iowa Farm Unity News*, January 1986).

The press and psychological counselors often worry that "depression" will result from loss of the land or the threat of it. But the word "depression" refers both to an internal state of despair and to an economic state of widespread unemployment and poverty. Infarm depression in the 1930s, unlike today, the land itself failed. What farmers face now, by contrast, is a more puzzling lack of connection between effort and reward, where productivity is high, but the money that products can bring in is very little. It is also significant that our contemporary psychological understanding of depression traces its cause to repressed anger. It may come as no surprise that the twin consequences of this particular depression in farmers can be suicide and murder. The pitchfork in Farmbo's hands could, after all, serve the same purpose as the machine gun in Rambo's.

What about the bankers? They are caught in a powerful bind. As capitalist enterprises, their banks must make a profit or go out of business. Marx and Polyani were at pains to point out that the ceaseless seeking of profit is required of capitalists: they must participate in it or their companies will be done in. One banker explained, "Last year, it was a wash, our losses offset earnings. But you can't survive if you just break even. We hope to make a profit this year" (Nordlinger 1985). But how to do this when the financial crisis in agriculture makes most loan applicants seem a poor risk? The result is the banker is prevented from "constantly throwing [his money] afresh into circulation": "We've got cash coming out of my ears . . . I'd like to lend but I've got to be careful" (Nordlinger 1985). On top of this, those the banker must deny money to "are like my brothers and sisters. . . . It's real easy to say yes and real tough to say no, but I have to do it more and more and more. I want to smile and help them, but I know I can't. It's as crushing as anything" (Nordlinger 1985).

This can help us see how the pressure on those denying the loans can be great too: some capitalists may be heartless, but others may experience as heartrending the abrogation of social responsibility the system some-times makes necessary. So it was for Mr. Litchfield, county supervisor for the Farm Home Administration, the farmer's lender of last resort. He had complained to his associates about

> restrictions on his ability—to help solve problems . . . a new and tougher agency policy on collections, announced Dec. 31, that followed a long period of forbearance resulting from a Federal court order. Under the new policy, borrowers with payments of more than $100 in arrears were being told they must bring their accounts up to date or face foreclosure proceedings. (Robbins 1986)

Leaving a note, "The job got pressure on my mind, left side, can't," on January 9, 1986, he is said to have shot his wife, two children, and the family dog in their sleep, then gone to his office and killed himself. In the midst of these events, the assessment of many people is summed up in this statment: "The general feeling of everybody I've talked to today is that his job killed him" (*New York Times*, January 10, 1986).

If nothing else, one thing is clear: these events do not represent eco-nomic actions carried on imperviously in their own sphere. Farmers and bankers alike struggle to come to terms with money and blood, life and death. A local newspaper summed it up: "the farm crisis is not numbers and deficits and bushels of corn. It is people and pride and tears and blood" (*Iowa City Press-Citizen*, December 10, 1985: A1). Or rather it is when numbers and deficits and bushels of corn are literally to be em-bodied in pride and tears and blood that tragic events occur. We saw earlier how the metaphors of production have "escaped their accustomed sphere" and found themselves in the domain of female reproduction and birth. Perhaps here is an even more sinister escape of a metaphor from one sphere to another. For we have not only corporate banks and farms—persons in the law—but also bankers and farmers—persons in flesh and blood—fighting to the death, lying on their death beds, making suicidal moves, and falling into the abyss.

Real as these struggles are for those who enact them, they can unfortunately serve as a kind of lightning rod, diverting public outrage away from the structural causes of the farm crisis and toward the need—legitimate enough—for psychological counseling. These causes (among them tax subsidies for big farm corporations and a weak balance of trade in agricultural commodities) are also being attacked directly. In one incident in Iowa a coalition of United Automobile Workers (builders of farm equipment) and family farmers, members of the Iowa Farm Unity Coalition, succeeded in stopping the auction of one farmer's machinery. His temporary reprieve in hand, the farmer asserted, "We're still on our land. I've known farmers to commit suicide in times like these, but I'm sure not gonna do that. The answer isn't in giving up. It's in uniting millions of workers and farmers" (*Iowa Farm Unity News*, December 1985).

Returning to John D. Rockefeller, he seemed certain the logic of the market was God's logic. In the small moments of life, for farmers and other citizens, this seems far from clear.

I ended my first lecture by mentioning three negative images that seem to attach to money processes in English and American literature. There was Shakespeare's consumption even to the point of eating the flesh of another person; Poe's connection between money and the horror of death; and Dickens' between wealth and fecal filth: in sum, cannibalism, death, and filth. In the meantime we saw how some of these themes worked out in China: pigs, money, and gold constituted ways women, young men, and local communities could achieve a modicum of autonomy against kinship structures or the state; resistances to the full flowering of capitalism were located in notions of usury and reprimands from Heaven, magical hedgehogs, and houses that lose their geomancy—and most of all in the domestication of money for social ends as its dual nature was bound within the same institutions. Death by suicide became another way of setting limits on the operation of money as the usurer was haunted by his debtor's ghost and as the "rotten fruit" of one who failed his or her obligations to a rotating credit society was driven to death or exile. Death by natural causes became, in the bone pots, another repository of value, and in the underworld, a further realm in which money and commodities (those "circulators") crossed between kin.

As for the United States, I have quoted several writers who agree with Tawney that our legacy is "a dualism which regards the secular and the religious aspects of life, not as successive stages within a larger unity, but as parallel and independent provinces, governed by different laws." In the cases we have looked at so far it seems to me people strive to bring the realm of morality, of meaning in life, together with the realm of the economy. In so doing, they often use images from the dark side of money (cannibalism, death, or filth), bringing them into arenas where economic forces and social concerns struggle:

- we have met a community struggling with Levitt, a Shylockian pig who literally consumes the flesh—the life savings—of other people;
- we have met farmers and bankers struggling with economic and psychological depression and enacting (embodying?) horrible deaths as their life careers seem to die or kill them;
- we have met women struggling to live with (and find other ways of describing) what science tells them is a monthly discharge of filthy menstrual waste, residue of unused materials, failed production.

I think it is less that our moral and economic provinces are separate and independent than that they clash in our lives most terribly. In my last lecture we will meet people who have tried to overcome the dissonance of this clash by literally giving the details of how money makes money the status of religious tenets and using them as moral principles by which to conduct their lives.

CHAPTER IV

Spirit and prosperity in the United States

In my first two lectures I argued that in China the two sides of money—its ability to enhance pure interaction and to encourage personal liberty—are held together in the same institutions, and tamed for social uses. In the third lecture we saw what happens when the side of money that erodes social bonds is set loose, and our struggles to contain it and live or die with its consequences. In this lecture we will see the coin, as it were, opened out and the attempt made to use it as an all-embracing meaning giver for life. In Western history, through the medieval period and up until late Puritanism, people tried to bring everything in their lives, economic and noneconomic, within a single moral compass. The people we will discuss today also strive to bring all within a single compass, but there has been a startling reversal: now laws of economic process have become an all-embracing religion that dictates relations among persons. The "general illumination" of capital has become a searing, all-encompassing radiance.

The New Life Clinic meets every Thursday morning in a Methodist church in Baltimore. This church, which otherwise has all the normal characteristics of Methodism, is located in an old residential neighborhood with an attached commercial center near the outskirts of the city limits. The Clinic was begun in 1950 by Ambrose and Olga Worrall, who had by that time become well known for their ability to heal people by the laying on of hands (Worrall and Worrall 1965). It is this practice that comprises the most central part of the Clinic's service in its present form, which otherwise consists of hymns, prayers, a Bible reading, and a sermon. For the laying on of hands, eight or ten healers form a line at the communion rail and the congregation then comes forward to meet them, roughly by row. Each healer places his or her hands on the kneeling person's head, shoulders, or other part of the body, holds them there for some moments of meditation, whispers a blessing, releases the person, and proceeds to the next.

A dominant theme in the service is the extent of fame the Clinic has achieved, which has brought much publicity to Ambrose and Olga. Films of the service have been made for the BBC series *Horizon* (and the PBS version, *Nova*), and Kirlian photographs of Olga's hands, made with a special process that shows the "aura" around them, have appeared in *Life* and *Smithsonian* magazines. This fame brings people from afar: one woman travels by bus every other week from Cleveland to attend the Clinic for her hypoglycemia and claims it is cheaper and more effective than her doctor; a family from Oregon flew to Baltimore to attend the service during Easter week; several people inevitably raise their hands each week when the minister of the church asks, "How many here from out of town?" and "How many here from out of the country?"

The impression I have from attending the services and lunches fairly regularly for more than a year is that many people who come to the Clinic believe they have been healed of some malady. One week at lunch I sat across from a woman whose hysterectomy and brain surgery had been canceled after a visit to the New Life Clinic when the doctor "could not find anything there"; another week, in the ladies' room, a woman said, flexing one arm, "I couldn't *move* my hand for two years and now it's healed"; Olga herself welcomed a mother and baby during the service, indicating that the mother's infertility had been healed at the Clinic. But many as those who claim to have been healed are, there are also plenty of people who are sick or maimed: adults and children bald from chemotherapy, blind, or otherwise disabled are not an uncommon sight in the congregation.

It is important to make clear that the tone and style of the service are extremely decorous. If anyone even threatens to lose control or make a scene, Olga, who has both the sweetness and the sternness of a rather firm grandmother, is quick to react. One week, a young man who obviously suffered from some mental impairment stood up and began to make noises. Olga immediately went to him and said loudly, "Young man, you stop that. We don't allow that here." The decorum of the service is no doubt related to the stratum of society from which most of the healers and congregation come. They are not "the half-baked, the uneducated, and the credulous" (Robert Laurence Moore 1977: 3). The healers who most frequently attend, for example, are two counselors from the University of Maryland medical school, a Quaker minister, a Presbyterian minister who is pastor to a wealthy suburban church, a former MD turned full-time writer and lecturer, and a Baptist minister. Occasional guest healers include a professor of theology from a seminary in an adjacent state and the chaplain of a local, private (and luxurious) mental institution. I have no systematic information on the income or occupation of the congregation, but the group is about four-fifths white and one-fifth black, and consistently well dressed. I have met no blue-collar workers but plenty of engineers, civil servants, college administrators, businessmen and -women, artists, and alternative health practitioners.

The dominant theme of the New Life Clinic is clearly the achievement of physical and mental health, often for those whom the medical profession has been unable to give much hope or help. I became aware of a subordinate theme, one that forms the focus of this talk, during one of minister Fred Orenschall's brief remarks during the first part of the service. In the most enthusiastic terms I had ever heard him use, he extolled the virtues of a book by Catherine Ponder, *Open Your Mind to Prosperity* (1971). I subsequently discovered that a large body of literature on the subject was on sale at the book table, some of it under the rubric "science of mind," and including various titles by Ponder, such as *Pray and Grow Rich* (1968) and *The Dynamic Laws of Prosperity: Forces That Bring Riches to You* (1962).

Prosperity, Ponder tells us, is governed by laws of the same sort as the natural laws that govern mathematics, music, physics, and all the other sciences (1962: 14–15). The "law of laws," as far as prosperity is concerned, is described as "radiation and attraction" or "supply and demand." This means that "what you radiate outward in your thoughts, feelings, mental pictures and words, you attract into your life and affairs" (1962: 15). Put otherwise, "you attract whatever you appreciate, and repel whatever you depreciate" (1962: 91). Applied to financial matters, this law yields the practical result that "if you think favorably about money, you multiply and increase it in your midst; whereas, if you criticize and condemn it in any form . . . you dissipate and repel it from you" (1962: 91).

In addition to thinking favorably about money, it is important to keep it in active circulation:

> Money is filled with the desire for life, movement, expansion and activity. It does not like to be grasped, clutched or restrained in idleness. Indeed, it is the active circulation of money that brings prosperity, whereas depressions and recessions are caused by the miserly hoarding of money. Even as our national economy depends upon the active circulation of money, so your individual prosperity depends upon the active circulation of money. (1962: 95)

Since the process of circulating money begins simply with positive thoughts about it, and since thought is available to anyone, it follows that no one need lack money. Poverty, then, is unnecessary, a sin, and "in its acute phases, it seems to be a form of insanity" (1962: 3).

The most abstract formulation Ponder gives for how thoughts can lead to money concerns the nature of "substance." "Substance" "stands under and supports every tangible and visible object" (1962: 100). It is filled with life, intelligence, and the ability to take tangible form. This is why Ponder says money is "divine," "filled with the intelligence of the universe," and "a God-given medium of exchange." When one gives substance one's attention, appreciation, and faith, it "manifests" itself as money or some other appropriate tangible form suited to one's needs. In this way one has control of the "invisible world of rich substance and rich supply, as well as the visible world of riches" (1962: 100). It is in the light of these principles that Pastor Orenschall closed a sermon at the New Life Clinic with a "meditation on prosperity": "I am not subject to market conditions because all of my affairs are directed by an all-knowing mind, forever opening up new sources of supply."

Substance will often manifest itself as money, but in its invisible form Ponder often describes it—metaphorically or literally, I am not sure—as gold dust. The introduction to *The Dynamic Laws* begins "There's Gold

Dust in the Air For You!" and elsewhere she makes "substance (gold dust, mind power)" equivalents for each other.

Ponder's books do not leave the matter of prosperity in the realm of these rather metaphysical arguments. They include plenty of practical advice about concrete steps one can take toward greater riches. Consider, for example, the Vacuum Law of Prosperity: "if you want great good, greater prosperity in your life, start forming a vacuum to receive it! In other words, get rid of what you don't want to make room for what you do want" (1962: 23). Ponder provides many examples of how this works. She herself once gave away two expensive velvet suits that no longer fit her. Within a week she received a letter from her sister saying that a lovely, extremely expensive velvet suit purchased abroad was on its way in the mail. Ponder comments,

> It arrived just in time to accompany me on my next trip, and its color even matched the auditorium in which I spoke. Furthermore, it was even more expensive than the suits I had just given away. That experience taught me that by giving up the expensive, one makes way for something even more beautiful to come, without financial stress. (1971: 24–25)

In addition to the Vacuum Law, there is the "secret of permanent prosperity": tithing one's income, preferably gross income, and preferably all channels of income.

> There is one basic problem in life: congestion. There is one basic solution: circulation. If your financial affairs have stagnated into indebtedness, hard times, and constant problems, you can clear up the congestion through beginning to trust God to help you, through your act of tithing to Him. *Tithing is an act of faith that brings about circulation and dissolves congestion.* (1971: 63, original emphasis)

Ponder provides numerous examples of the immediate and dramatic improvements in one's finances that follow correct tithing.

Another practical method, listed under the heading "Techniques for Becoming Financially Independent," is to mentally multiply your money by ten. For example, if you have $5 in your wallet, look at it and declare: "I give thanks that ten times this much or $50 is now on its way to me and quickly manifests in perfect ways" (1962: 127). For those who are advanced in this technique, Ponder suggests thinking your money is multiplied by 100: either technique will give you "freedom from the thought of lack, poverty and 'not enough'! It completely changes your attitude to: 'This is a rich universe and there's plenty for you and for me'" (1962: 129).

A closely related technique is to image money with the aid of play money. A salesman who was having hard times carried play money in his wallet. Every night he would take out bills in denominations of $50 or $100, hold them in his hands, and look at them for some time. As he increased his daily sales, he increased the denominations of the bills he carried and looked at, until finally he was carrying and looking at bills of $10,000 and $20,000. In another case, which illustrates Ponder's view of how poverty should be dealt with, a "domestic worker informed her employer that she needed more money for daily living. Her employer told her to get some play money to help her think definitely about prosperity" (1964: 100). The employer gave her maid $5 in play money, and subsequently she found a $5 bill on the street, which enabled her to buy a new uniform (1964: 100)!

As a chapter in American history, this treatment of paper money has come almost full circle. We began by treating faith in paper money as a patriotic act—during the War of Revolution only paper money, continental dollars, was used as money within the states, all available specie being needed to buy war materials from foreign countries (Newman 1967: 13). Refusal to accept paper money in payment was taken as treason. One hundred years later, at the end of the nineteenth century, there was a strong movement against reliance on paper money as being an insubstantial fiction (Wells 1896). With Ponder we return to faith in paper money, even play money, where pure form without substance can be given all the substance it needs in the realm of thought.

Perhaps the most elaborate practical method Ponder recommends for increasing prosperity is making a "wheel of fortune" or a "modern prayer wheel." You begin by outlining a circle on a large piece of poster board and dividing it into the various departments of your life: financial, job, health, family, and so on. You then paste pictures on the board representing your desired good for each category. Finally you should hide your board and keep it secret from others, but view it yourself every day, preferably just before sleeping. Some further hints for success: use big, colorful boards if you want big, colorful results in your life (a college professor made a small, crowded, drab, colorless wheel of fortune for travel abroad and he had a crowded, drab, colorless trip); do not clutter your wheel of fortune (a housewife placed a small, crowded house on her wheel and got just that); be sure to put money on the board, not just the things you want ("otherwise you may get the things, plus indebtedness! [You can use 'play money,' also checks on the board]") (Ponder 1971: 86–87).

Ponder gives a great many examples of how successful wheels of fortune can be, among them the story of a "tenement family." An overworked housewife, mother of nine children, and living in a slum tenement, was dependent on the inadequate wages her husband made as a day laborer. When she learned about wheels of fortune, she made one showing her husband in a well-paying job, the family in a large, comfortable house with outdoor space and a car. "When the prayer wheel began to work," Ponder tells us, her husband was offered a job overseeing a ranch, which included a nice house, a car, and hundreds of acres of ranchland for the children to play on (1968: 165–66).

When I first encountered the prosperity ideas of Catherine Ponder I had no idea that they extended beyond her books on the book table at the New Life Clinic, Fred Orenschall's sermons, and people at New Life Clinic lunches who carried "Pray and Prosper" booklets with them. I could hardly have been more naïve. The motherlode of these ideas lies elsewhere. First there is the enormous publishing company, Science of Mind Publications, which, in addition to numerous books and pamphlets, puts out a monthly magazine called *Science of Mind*. Second there is the Unity Church, whose Baltimore center sells literally dozens of books, cassette tapes, and pamphlets on prosperity, not only by Catherine Ponder but by half a dozen other authors as well, and in addition offers classes on prosperity every Monday night.

Unity had its historical roots in the American metaphysical movement of the late nineteenth century. For a while it was a part of the New Thought Alliance, but in the early part of the twentieth century it broke off on its own (Myer 1965: 23). Drawing on the mind cure philosophy, New Thought saw men as individualizations of God. Although they were not identical to God, nothing could hamper their communication with God when the person's mind was properly attuned. Once in contact with universal knowledge (God), man could draw forth anything he wished to know, and this is one instance of what was meant by "supply" (Myer 1965: 59). To answer the question how mind could affect matter, mind cure theorists came up with an intermediate substance called "spiritual matter." Healing took place as mind affected this spiritual matter, which in turn affected the body. This "matter" consisted of a storehouse of past experiences, thoughts, ideas, mental pictures. It could be culled over and, as it was "exposed to Truth, the erroneous, faulty, disease-producing, worry-inducing items [would be] eliminated" (Myer 1965: 71).

The founders of Unity, Charles and Myrtle Fillmore, began publishing their ideas in a small magazine in 1889. Today Unity publications include three English-language magazines with a subscription of almost two million and translations into eight languages, and scores of books brought to ten thousand readers through Unity Book Club (Freeman 1978: 215–16). Unity headquarters are in Kansas City, where Unity Village occupies 1400 acres, and Unity school and seven Unity centers stand nearby (1978: 219).

Seen in the light of the wider Unity literature, Ponder certainly represents the most flamboyant advocate of prosperity thinking. However, the basic tenants of her program are all contained in the writings of the Fillmores and echoed in other authors' books (Fillmore 1936; Russell 1950), such as the enormously prolific and popular Orison Swett Marden, who published in the 1920s. One author, Eric Butterworth, has published a new book which is especially liked at the Baltimore Unity Center because, I was told, "it keeps prosperity thinking on a spiritual plane." Butterworth makes easily identifiable references to Ponder's ideas as "gross," "sickening" materializations of "a beautiful spiritual truth" (1983: 184). In his version of these ideas, "The goal should be not to make money or acquire things, but to achieve the consciousness through which the substance will flow forth when and as you need it" (1983: 16). It is no less acceptable to Butterworth than to Ponder to attain material wealth, but one should attain it through "consciousness of ever-present substance," which, like a magnetic force, will draw things to you (1983: 43–44).

There are many connections between prosperity and healing. For some authors, prosperity denotes a general state of well-being, in which one experiences freedom from financial worries, good physical health, peace, and harmony (Butterworth 1983: vii). In general, good physical health is attained the same way wealth is, by filling one's mind with positive thoughts about harmony and right functioning. Sometimes, more explicit causal connections are drawn between one's wealth and health, especially the circulation of wealth and circulation within the body.

> The substance that comprises your mind, body and affairs constantly seeks to express its life as activity in you and in your world. When allowed to do so consistently through the rhythmetic law of giving and receiving, order fills your mind, harmony fills your body and affairs, abundant good fills your world. If you do not allow the substance of the universe to flow through your mind, body and affairs systematically, you get out of balance with the pulsating rhythm of the universe. Congestion and imbalance follow. (Ponder 1966: 205)

Specifically, when you allow your thoughts about money to be stiff, hard, and unyielding, your arteries also become stiff, hard, and unyielding. You will be told you have hardening of the arteries, but "the arteries that hardened first were the main arteries leading to and from [your] seldom-opened pocketbook!" (Ponder 1966: 206). The solution is to make your money-substance circulate through tithing. One man testified that his first tithe "took away a strange circulatory ailment which defied medical help" (Ponder 1971: 63).

It seems to me that prosperity theory accurately represents aspects of the capitalist economy in the United States. The constant emphasis on the beneficial effects of circulation of substance and the disastrous effects of stagnation seems to relate to the fact that money does have to circulate through the economy in order to make more money. Some early prosperity thinkers had teachers who knew from direct experience how this worked. Ralph Waldo Trine, for example, made a pilgrimage to see Henry Ford. Although Ford said he had read and been sustained by Trine's work, he proceeded to let Trine know he had misunderstood the operation of capital. As against Trine's admonitions to save, Ford insisted people ought only to spend. "Society lives by circulation and not by congestion (Myer 1965: 198). To make his point, he rewrote an ad the company was using – "Buy a Ford and save the difference" – to read "Buy a Ford and spend the difference"!

Underlying the concern with circulation is a clear notion that when money goes out to circulate, it will return bringing more money. It is an ideology, not of giving and receiving, not of gifts going out and when they return bringing an obligation to give again, but of giving out and receiving more than one gave. Catherine Ponder's suits, which she gave away only to receive even more expensive ones, and play money that makes real money multiply, both illustrate aspects of Marx's famous formulas, $M–C–M'$, $C–C'$, and $M–M'$ (1967, I: 155).

The way prosperity theorists talk about money making money captures very well the autonomous character money seem to us to have, its occult quality of spontaneously generating itself and automatically expanding. As we saw last time, here again money "has acquired the occult quality of being able to add value to itself. It brings forth living offspring, or, at the least, lays golden eggs" (Marx 1967, I: 154). In these idioms, the process of capital production seems to be a property inherent in commodities and in money.

Prosperity thinkers also see the process of capital production as the result of the interaction of money with money or commodities with commodities, not as the result of social interactions. Suits go out, leaving a "vacuum" which attracts better suits, and images on fortune wheels attract all manner of things, without the involvement of any social relationship. The only thing that is necessary for the accumulation of wealth is solitary thought and imagery. Because of their eliding of the social relationships that are involved in the production of wealth, prosperity thinkers can see poverty as a condition that can be fixed without any change in social relationships or any change in the allocation of resources among persons. In one case Ponder cites, a man got into dire financial straits by giving money to a needy relative. Giving money to a poor relative will cause stagnation in the donor's affairs and keep the recipient in poverty: "It is far wiser to give him literature on how to use the laws of prosperity for himself. This will prosper him permanently, and make him independent of poverty programs or handouts" (1971: 63–64).

This kind of remark about poverty does not, I believe, result from callousness. Prosperity theorists often assert that there is more than enough substance for everyone to prosper. "There may be many 'pockets of poverty' in the world, and countless victims of deprivation. However, the Truth is, despite the appearance of great lack, in every area, in every human life, there is an infinite and eternal energy from which all things proceed so you shouldn't be poor" (Butterworth 1983: 6). As Charles Fillmore, the cofounder of Unity put it, in the new era made possible by prosperity thinking, there "will be no place for lack. Supply will be more equalized. There will not be millions of bushels of wheat stored in musty warehouses while people go hungry. There will be no inequalities of supply, for God's substance will be recognized and used by all people" (Fillmore 1936: 23). Throughout these writings, the assertion is made repeatedly that "supply is unlimited"; poverty is caused only by "lack of flow and circulation."

Like these authors' picture of how money makes money, this picture of how poverty can be overcome is partly accurate and partly false. Anyone who has looked at a chart of social stratification in the United States with information on the extremely unequal distribution of income and wealth would probably agree with Butterworth and Fillmore that supply is unlimited! Most would probably also agree that poverty would be eliminated if money and goods circulated differently. But the kind of change I, for one, would envision being necessary is that control over the means of production would have to be redistributed, which in turn would lead to changes in the basis on which money and goods circulate. Prosperity theorists, blinded, as Marx would say, by the "fantastic form" they give money and commodities, do not see what changes in social relations, what social action, would have to occur in order for supply to circulate freely throughout the population. For them, it is sufficient to believe that supply is unlimited. In fact, the reason our country is as rich as it is, they claim, is that many of us do have "prosperity consciousness." "If we were all in a poverty consciousness, famines would be as common here as they are in India or China. . . . The burden of the poverty thought reacts on the earth so that year after year it withholds its products and many people starve" (Fillmore 1936: 90).

Treating money and commodities as if they somehow automatically created more wealth is a form of what Marx called fetishism, treating creations of the human brain as if they were "independent beings endowed with life and entering into relation both with one another and the human race" (1967, I: 72). In other words, what are really things are treated as if they were persons. The opposite, but inseparably connected other side of this process is depersonalization, in which other people are treated instrumentally, as things or abstract means, rather than as whole persons (1967, I: 105).

I have wondered a lot about whether the Unity Church or the New Life Clinic depersonalizes human relationships. This is a complicated question, and I do not yet feel confident of the answer. The remarks I have already cited about how the poor should prosper themselves certainly do not encourage active involvement in the particular circumstances of others' lives, but neither are adherents of prosperity thought disinterested in others' circumstances. Similarly, the familiar Christian emphasis on "loving thy neighbor" takes the following form in prosperity literature: when divine love (another word for substance) is manifest in a person, hateful thoughts such as resentment, criticism, sorrow, remorse, guilt, fear, anger, and jealousy are changed into life thoughts (Ponder 1966: 122). The result desired is harmony within the self and with other people, but this is never attained through interaction with others, only through internal thought. In this sense, whatever is going on in the lives or emotions of other people essentially escapes notice. In a real sense, they might as well be things. Historically, for early prosperity thought writers, the significant relationships in the economy and society were not between men, that is, they were not personal, whether in conflict or cooperation. They were between men and the pattern of all things, the laws, the infinite (Myer 1965: 95).

The idea of sectarian groups that see themselves as religious and identify themselves with Christianity, and yet stress the virtues of wealth and ignore the condition of other human beings, is quite shocking to me, doubtless because I have come to accept our culture's dominant view of what the Christian religion is. There is indirect evidence that prosperity theorists are aware of this dominant view and feel a need to justify the way they diverge from it: they have undertaken a massive rewriting of Christianity's sacred texts. Under the series title "The Millionaires of the Bible," several Catherine Ponder volumes have appeared: *The Millionaires of Genesis* (1976), *The Millionaire Moses* (1977), *The Millionaire Joshua* (1978), and *The Millionaire from Nazareth* (1979). Some of the most plausible reinterpretations refer to Jesus' miracles as evidence that "he was at one with all interior and exterior wealth": "A wonder-working mind that could turn ordinary water into the finest of wine, multiply bread and fish at will to feed thousands, raise the dead to life, and heal all manner of disease could hardly be counted poor—especially if these invaluable services were being performed at today's prices!" (Ponder 1979: 2).

Some of the least plausible—to me, at any rate—include the claim that Jesus had nothing against luxurious living: after all he dined with those of wealth such as the Pharisees, Zacchaeus, or Mary of Bethany, and while dining with Mary, he allowed his feet to be anointed with precious oils (Ponder 1979: 15); his seamless robe was, according to Orenschall, "the equivalent of a $500 Brooks Brothers suit," so valuable that the Roman soldiers bartered for it.

Then there is the rewritten 23rd Psalm:

> The Lord is my banker; my credit is good.
> He maketh me to lie down in the consciousness
>   of omnipresent abundance;
> He giveth me the key to his strongbox.
> He restoreth my faith in his riches;
> He guideth me in the paths of prosperity for
>   His name's sake.
> Yes, though I walk in the very shadow of debt,
> I shall fear no evil, for Thou are with me;
> Thy silver and Thy gold they secure me.
> Thou preparest a way for me in the presence of
>   the collector;
> Thou fillest my wallet with plenty; my measure
>   runneth over.
> Surely goodness and plenty will follow me all
>   the days of my life,
> And I shall do business in the name of the Lord forever.
> (Quoted in Huber 1971: 313)

It is probably no accident that Charles Fillmore, the cofounder of Unity, was a man who repeatedly tried to make it rich as a small investor in real estate and mining. According to his biographer, he experienced numerous boom and bust cycles in towns in Colorado, Nebraska, and Kansas from 1879 to 1889 (Freeman 1978: 37–40). (Parenthetically,

Lewis Henry Morgan's main investment, a blast furnace, also went bankrupt during one of these busts [Resek 1960: 109]). It is surely also no accident that during these years, in contrast to Fillmore, other businessmen in the United States, such as Rockefeller, Carnegie, Morgan, Gould, and so on, were amassing gigantic fortunes (Zinn 1980: 247–52). In general the years between 1860 and 1900 were ones of many business panics: "firms were failing at the rate of 100 or worse to every 10,000 firms and even the Titans of this felt insecure. Rockefeller spoke of the hazardous and perilous oil business and Carnegie of being 'overwhelmed by business cares'" (Kirkland 1956: 9).

This combination of the possibility of enormous wealth together with high risk in attaining it might well add to rather than detract from prosperity theory's appeal. The greater the success of some corporations, and the greater the risk of failure of others, the more it must seem that "supply" in the universe *is* ample, if only one could find the way to get it. Most people "are pinching their supply by stepping upon the hose through which plenty would come to them" (Marden, quoted in Huber 1971: 155). Using another metaphor, Marden goes on:

> We go through life using a little eight candle power bulb, believing we are getting all the power that can come to us, all that we can express or that destiny will give us, believing that we are limited to eight candle power bulbs. We never dream that an infinite current, a current in which we are perpetually bathed would flood our lives with light, with a light inconceivably brilliant and beautiful, if we would only put on a larger bulb, make a larger connection with the infinite supply current. (1917: 216)

Under conditions of relatively untrammeled competition, when over half of the population were independent entrepreneurs, one might even guess that an ideology like prosperity thought would arise. In the contemporary United States, this ideology might seem to be an anachronism, especially if one imagines that the domination of monopoly capital has meant the demise of the independent entrepreneur (Braverman 1974: 404). In fact, however, of the twelve million business enterprises in the United States, all but a few thousand are small or medium-size businesses, and well over eleven million can be classified as entrepreneurial firms (Edwards 1979: 34). The amount of franchising and subcontracting engaged in by large corporations may in fact be swelling the numbers of firms in entrepreneurial situations. And as in the late nineteenth century, the failure rate is extremely high, as is the rate of incorporation of new businesses (*Small Business Administration Annual Reports*). What has happened is that these firms exist on the periphery of the economy, dominated by monopoly corporations, and even more constrained in their activities than their counterparts were in the nineteenth century: giant corporations can now dictate whom they sell to, whom they buy materials from, and ultimately, especially if they are successful, who owns them (Edwards 1979: 72–73).

If one sought a correlation between similar economic settings and surges of interest in prosperity literature, it would not be difficult to show that we are currently experiencing a great renewal of interest in this literature. Titles available two years ago only from obscure mail-order companies have been reissued and they and many new publications are on sale at national book store chains like B. Dalton. Ads for prosperity thought publications are appearing in entrepreneurial magazines, such as this *Financial Independence*, directed to Black businesses. Television has financial prophets who dominate Sunday morning programming on some channels. In some areas cable TV is almost entirely dominated by these prophets of capitalism: current estimates are that 40 percent of the nation's TV households or sixty-one million Americans have at least minimal exposure to them (Ostling 1986: 63) and mail-order prosperity is flourishing. My favorite such prophet is the Rev. Ewing, from whom I have received twelve communications so far, each with an object I am supposed to use in a certain way and then return to start the flow of wealth, health, and happiness. The objects include a shower cap, a handkerchief, a Mexican peso, a five peso bill from the Japanese occupation of the Philippines to be used as a "seed," and a prosperity cross—all of which are said to bring spiritual, physical, and financial blessings.

A new strain of writing has also joined the ranks. Former devotees of communal living and Eastern spiritualism are now embracing prosperity thought. Having rejected money before to avoid its individuating aspects, they are now embracing it to capture its social interactive aspects. "Money may most usefully be viewed as a symbol of energy. Money stands for energy that passes between us. It is not a thing but a transaction, a transfer, an exchange" (Fields 1984: 128). But money itself is not used to connect people in this new version any more than it is in the original literature:

> When we feel guilty because we think there are poor people in the world
> . . . we associate this with money, because money is the conceptual con-
> nection that links us to the so-called poor. For example, parents in the
> United States perennially refer to "the poor people in China who are hun-
> gry" . . . the only real relationship between people in China and us is at a
> cosmic level. The real relation we have with them has nothing to do with
> the amount of money we have in our bank accounts or the amount that
> some Chinese have in yuans' worth of cattle. (Phillips 1974: 154)

Some of the new spread of prosperity thought is almost entirely secular, in which the influence of thought on material wealth is kept, but reference to God drops out. This passes into the category of "success literature" generally, as in tapes for self-hypnosis or in "success" charts, which show you "the attitudes that lead to success and the attitudes that lead to failure." "Look at it every day, See the difference it can make in your life. See the strange and subtle motivation that it has on your life" (*Success Magazine*, February 1986: 79).

If prosperity thought represents a folk model of the economy, perhaps it does so from the vantage point of the small investor or small businessman, on whom certain costs of capitalism bear quite heavily: the necessity of taking investment risks, where failure may mean bankruptcy. One recent article on franchises warns the franchisee: "Remember you are taking all the risk" (Cornell 1985). Then there is the inevitability of experiencing low points in the business cycle, where lack of diversification or inadequate reserves also mean bankruptcy; the relative difficulty of obtaining capital and credit from lenders (Boone and Kurtz 1976: 526–27). Although I have no exact figures on the occupations of members of the New Life Clinic or Unity Christianity, many of the people I have met there share with Fillmore experience of the extremely high failure rate of small businesses (Schabacker 1971: 36). They could surely appreciate his plaintive remarks: "For many of us there is either a feast or a famine in the matter of money and we need the abiding consciousness. There is no reason why we should not have a continuous even flow of substance both in income and outgo" (Fillmore 1936: 20).

To me it is ironic and more than a little sad that the program of "action" that prosperity theorists advocate to overcome the very real costs suffered by small businessmen and investors involves only individual thought. If our "collective consciousness" is one of prosperity, if our individual thoughts are "bullish," the whole economy can be turned around. "For the sake of mankind as a whole, as well as for your own experience, think substance, think prosperity, think plenty for all" (Butterworth 1983: 212).

It may be that prosperity thought replicates the viewpoint of the small business or franchise in its late-nineteenth- or early-twentieth-century version. Or it may be it reflects a more general condition. John Kenneth Galbraith points out that the economy is now entirely on a non-metallic standard, and has been since the Second World War (1975: 136; see also Harvey 1982: 244). Occasionally economists discuss the possibility of returning to a metallic standard, only to realize that no one really knows how to do this. Our entire economy is based on faith in paper money, stocks, bonds, credit, and checks. So with the intensity of faith here, prosperity thought may make great sense: "If you gotta have faith, you might as well have faith."

As a way of encapsulating my view of prosperity thought, let me turn to Habermas, who describes the difference between crises in early, or liberal, capitalism, and late, or state-regulated, capitalism. In early capitalism, "the accumulation of total capital is achieved by way of periodic devaluations of certain parts of it" (Habermas 1973: 364). This produced the boom and bust cycles of the late nineteenth and early twentieth centuries experienced by Fillmore, Marden, and other prosperity thinkers.

In late capitalism, two major changes occur: the state has stepped in to regulate the market; and economic enterprises become more concentrated. (National and multinational corporations dominate the scene.) Habermas sees a new kind of crisis developing in late capitalism, a crisis of legitimation. This occurs, he argues, because "taken-for-granted cultural factors which previously were fringe conditions of the political system are now drawn into the administrative field of planning" (1973: 377–78). He means that in education, for example, in the past school authorities only codified a tradition that had developed spontaneously and had its own community-based legitimacy. Now, however, "the planning of the curriculum is based on the premise that the patterns provided by tradition could be otherwise constituted" (1973: 378).

The same process is going on in land ownership (regional and town planning), health (hospitals), family (family planning, marriage laws), and socialization (preschool education). Once these traditional areas are "startled out of their spontaneous development," the unquestionableness of their tradition has been destroyed and they are not available as a source of legitimacy. The crisis faced by late capitalist systems, then, is how to secure legitimation in grounds that have the aura of "the unquestionable"?

What success and prosperity thought apparently show us is that the source of legitimation of a system need not lay outside it. For them the principles by which the system operates have been lifted to the level of a principle of divine truth. Ironically enough this has been done by those experiencing the competitive fringe around monopolies and therefore who reap few of the total profits and many of the costs (Baran and Sweezy 1966).

Let me try to pull a few things together by drawing a series of contrasts between our two cases.

In China we saw that usurious practices were regarded as contrary to the nature of society and that they were construed as a warning from Heaven—in other words, cosmic forces supported social needs. In the nineteenth-century United States we saw that usury was welcomed by some as a law of nature— in other words, cosmic forces supported the market.

In China we saw suicides occurring because when a person could not reliably repay money it was taken as a failure of his or her social links to others—in other words, personhood was constituted by social linkages. In the US farm depression, we saw suicide and murder occurring because when a person could not repay a debt it was taken as a failure of his or her ability to be a productive worker—in other words personhood was constituted by one's ability to produce and own commodities.

In China we saw women—jurally disadvantaged persons—benefiting from the liberatory aspects of money in their unique ability to hold it privately. In the United States we saw women jurally disadvantaged here too—injured still further by the ways their bodies were imaged medically with models of production that seeped through from another sphere.

In China we saw pigs as depositories of household resources deliberately used to cause "congestion" in the flow of funds out to the state. In the United States we saw Levitt, an "irrational capitalist" who "ate" more from the trough than he was entitled to, subjected to intense moral and legal discipline.

In China we saw, in addition to earthly exchange, another realm of exchange with the spirit world, where spirit money and paper commodities could again cross between kin, linking them even after death. In the United States we also saw a second realm of money use among prosperity thinkers, where in isolated private contemplation of play money or paper images of commodities they imagined specific increments to their "supply." Summing it all up, in China we saw the many roads across which money and objects traveled among people, creating and renewing exchange and interdependence. In the United States we saw the single road to success (in the success chart) traveled by isolated individuals and surrounded by isolated pitfalls at every turn.

In *The Gift*, Marcel Mauss says,

> We live in a society where there is a marked distinction . . . between persons and things. This distinction is fundamental; it is the very condition of part of our system of property, alienation and exchange. But are these distinctions not of relatively recent appearance in the codes of the great civilizations? Did not those civilizations pass through a previous phase in which their thought was less cold and calculating? Did not they themselves at one time practice these customs of gift-exchange in which persons and things become indistinguishable? (1967: 46)

As Jonathan Parry points out in his 1985 Malinowski Lecture, in the modern West, gift exchange, in which persons and things are not clearly separated, is fractured. For us, gifts seem opposed to market exchange, persons to things, interest to disinterest. We have an ideology that makes us think the "pure realm" of altruistic, moral relations is separate from the corrupt realm of cold calculating market relations.

Last time we saw that despite this ideology, in practice, market relations as people experience them are thoroughly imbued with moral relations; today we saw the attempt to use market relations themselves as a moral compass. In my view this attempt runs afoul of significant contradictions, and it may be that any efforts to use market relations as if they could give moral significance to life will do the same. Consider, for example, the use being made of gold as a symbol in the media. In the realm of pure exchange, finance banking and investments, transactions depend to a large degree on mutual trust, promises that can be depended on and tacit acceptance of a common code of conduct (Neale 1976: 60). This kind of trust, caught in the image of gold as it is associated with high finance, can be juxtaposed to and claimed to give meaning to the intimate realm of personal relationships. To see how hollow the effort is, we could consider a recent series of ads focused on gold and linking trust to banking, love to a woman's heart. In China we saw gold as treasure, as a precipitate of preexisting dense webs of interconnections. In the United States we see gold as an aspect of the "general illumination" of capital masquerading as if possessing it meant we were loved and giving it away meant we loved.

Perhaps Morgan experienced similar contradictions, as an investor who used his profits to finance his studies of groups (Native Americans) whose dire circumstances were a product of other investors' desire for land and resources. Or as a capitalist whose philanthropies to women's education (Resek 1960: 56) could contribute to mitigating some inequalities created by the very system that was the source of his wealth. In his desire to avoid the consequences of a "mere property career," Morgan deserves to be heard again here at the end, in the ominous prophecies that close *Ancient Society*: "A mere property career is not the final destiny of mankind, if progress is to be the law of the future as it has been of the past. . . . The dissolution of society bids fair to become the termination of a career of which property is the end and aim; because such a career contains the elements of self-destruction" (1877: 552).

Another way of putting what I have tried to suggest about our two cases is that in China, through rotating credit societies and marriage, what for us seem to be two separate realms are bound together; and so the destructive effects of money are tamed. In the US case, prosperity thought and success literature show us examples of how in the logic of market relations the ideology of money as capital can be loosed from any bounds, and perhaps out of desperation the attempt can be made to cast this as an all-encompassing, meaning-giving net capturing all spheres of life. Perhaps they are grasping for the "pure interaction," "congealed exchange," that money actually does represent, as a way to get more sense of interconnectedness with others in the desolate isolation of modern society. In my view the pathos in this is that money as a way to interconnect can be a mirage unless it is accompanied by other forms of social interaction. "The abstract form of the moral order [has been taken] for its living substance" (Nelson 1949: 135).

Maybe the danger prosperity thinkers fall prey to is the illusion that nothing does lie outside the "general illumination" of capital. Perhaps this is the "element of self-destruction" in Morgan's prophecy. If that were so, we might as well join prosperity thinkers in letting the illumination take on the radiance of religious truth.

Given my usual penchant for finding resistance and awareness everywhere, I find myself pretty stumped by prosperity thinkers. The only area I can construe as resistance is their views on labor. As you may have realized already, the link they make between purely mental labors and wealth completely avoids the need to work in the usual sense. While this might seem a shocking departure from sacrosanct American beliefs in the necessity of labor (Rodgers 1974: 126), it would be more accurate to see it as a rejection of the drudgery of manual labor and an embracing of mental labor. Henry H. Brown's 1903 tract *Dollars Want Me* is dedicated "To All Who Would Be Free from the Grind of Labor" and begins: "It will help you rise above the drudgery of enforced labor and enable you to enter upon the manifold expressions of life with the joy and spontaneity of childhood" (1903: 5–6). With the development of capitalism a purely mental realm of labor is actually created (management) and takes to itself a disproportionate share of rewards (Braverman 1974); prosperity thinkers are, reasonably enough, trying to emulate this sector.

But even in their views of work, I do think prosperity thinkers are operating within the terms of the system. Like the workers during the industrial revolution described by E. P. Thompson (1967), who first struggled against new notions of time and later accepted them, then using them to their own advantage as best they could, these people are not struggling against the forces of a new system; they are using the terms of the system to try to better their own lot. They have accepted that persons are isolated monadic individuals, and that wealth and power come from throwing money ever fresh into circulation. The most that can be said is that they are trying to coax money to flow along lines it usually does not—that is, to themselves.

However, I am not really discouraged by finding that these people have decided to play the game and win by its rules. For alternative visions of the world to develop, it is probably necessary for people to perceive accurately the workings of the ones they are in. I am continually amazed by the richness of the ways people manage to do this. We have seen examples in the homely but compelling Chinese images of hedgehogs and houses, developed on the brink of capitalism; and perhaps prosperity thought does some of this, in the ways it images the necessity for a continuous flow of money, or the links it makes between health in the body and money in society.

The ground on which people stand to launch a critique of the system is the ground of their own lives, as they experience and struggle with complex forces. These struggles are to be found nearly everywhere we look: in the inchoate feeling that something is not right about selling a doll bought for a child; in silences—the refusal of some women to talk about medical views of their bodies; in organized collective groups such as the alliance between factory workers and farmers happening in the Midwest. As I look at all this my mood becomes, not discouraged, but somber, as in Barrington Moore's "becoming really serious about a very deadly and very serious world" (1972: 193). However great the difficulties of seeing, as Moore puts it, "the range of possibilities in a future that always carries on its back the burden of the present and the past" (1972: 193), I still have a lot of hope that a more satisfying and just basis for human community can someday be conceived and realized.

Afterword

We, the authors of this afterword,[1] belong to different intellectual generations. This difference, our ongoing conversations, and our exchanges with Emily Martin all frame our combined reflections on these Morgan Lectures. We take note of the time that these lectures were written and delivered (1986), and then suggest how their new availability, in widely accessible forms, invites new conversations: across disciplines, in comparative studies, and in the advancing analytics of the study of money. We expect that younger generations will connect to this work through even more lines of inquiry, for their research of novel practices in the emergent, interconnected world differs so profoundly from the world of 1986—a moment when modern western capitalism was still the main theoretical model *of* the modern economy and provided models *for* expansive practices in "the market economy," as communist economies became troubled in various ways and started to connect more broadly to the global economy. The ambitious thinking in these lectures aimed not only to bring one of the most important and longest-lasting monetized economies on the globe into the comparative repertoire, but also to introduce new analytics that are even more relevant today, as the study of

---

1. Although this afterword is jointly authored, the two different voices identify each of us as primary author of a section: Mintz looking back, Guyer speaking to the present.

money and moral economy rapidly expands its geographical, historical, analytical, and anticipatory horizons.

LOOKING BACK TO 1986

Filling in the background on how she composed her Morgan Lectures, Emily Martin paints an evocative and lively account of life from nearly four decades ago in Johns Hopkins' Anthropology Department. Her reminiscence fits well with my own memories of those years, meanwhile awakening yet other recalls. Generations of past research in economic anthropology are brought to mind, both through memories of personal encounters, and through surviving texts.

Now as I look back to 1975 and what followed, it was not—it seems to me—that we who were involved had been such great planners. But from my perch, the spirit of my junior colleagues was so fresh and daring, the readiness to help each other, students and faculty both, so palpable, that it honestly was a daily joy to come to work. For a great many years we faculty members were becoming more educated ourselves, simply by virtue of educating our students as our equals. Martin makes clear that we did so in the company of many eminent and inspiring colleagues, to whom all of us juniors will remain forever in debt.

Now, as I read Martin's lectures, I am struck to find how much she learned from Karl Polanyi while she was crafting them. His work was inspirational for many anthropologists interested in the economies of other societies and examining broad comparative and historical cases, as well as particular ethnographic examples. Polanyi's books and papers are now enjoying a well-deserved revival, and all I can say is that it could not have happened to a more relevant thinker (or for that matter, to a nicer guy).

I got to know Polanyi only slightly. It was around the time that I was finishing my graduate training at Columbia. I had taken my first job and it was out of New York City; but I still came to the city frequently. Polanyi had a chair at Columbia. When I first met him, however, he was no longer giving formal classes there. Yet he was a familiar sight on the

Columbia campus; and once you had seen and heard Polanyi, you were not likely to forget him.[2]

He gave quite a few public lectures in those years. I remember him explaining at one such meeting that while trade, the marketplace, and a medium of exchange (money) may all be present in a society, none of them, nor even all three together, makes a society capitalistic. A capitalistic society has a "self-regulating market," in his words. It is not a market *place*, nor need it be one. It is, rather, an economic process by which all the factors of production, including producers' goods, and land, and money, and labor, are endowed with their prices, as if by magic. It is the market, and only the market, that tells us what those prices are.

Polanyi is probably best known among non-economists for his simple assertion that in a capitalist society, social relations are embedded in the economy; while in a non-capitalist society economic relations are embedded in the society. This is the view that undergirds Martin's analysis of her Chinese and U.S. data. But Polanyi argues that land and especially labor *cannot* be considered commodities like others (such as capital goods) because of their intrinsic nature—qualities that they had and could never lose entirely, before being transformed into commodities.

Obviously the economic life of humans did not begin with capitalism. It was about 2.6 million years ago that hominids of one or more species systematically began to modify stone surfaces on a regular basis

---

2. He had to travel to New York City from Canada to teach. His wife, Ilona, a member of the Canadian Communist Party, was forbidden to enter the United States. At the time I made his acquaintance, he was coming down each week or two to meet with several of his students and ex-students in a modest Morningside Heights apartment. The class was conducted in the evening, on the chairs and floor of the living room, while Polanyi held forth from the couch. An excellent lecturer and a fine wrangler, he loved to argue. I clearly recall sitting next to him one night when he leaned across me to speak to a student, while another class member was holding forth. "When he finishes," he whispered, "you take the affirmative and leave me the negative." He was inspiring up close, the way that all good teachers hope to be. I was able to attend only a few times—since I was teaching in New Haven—but each time it was hugely exciting. Polanyi was always dressed formally but comfortably, by which I mean he wore a jacket and tie, but would push the tie aside from time to time in order to scratch himself inside his generously large shirt collar.

in order to make tools. Such cultural activity, leading over time to the establishment of craft traditions, was based upon intelligent human effort, the active implementation of human intentions. Such activity was not instinctive, hormonally determined. As Marx argued, the human doers *thought of* what they did before they did it. When we speak of labor, we understand that for hundreds of millennia, labor (among other things) had no price. More recently, in the feudal era, labor might become a specific unit of effort, embodied in the prices of products that were set by guilds. But only with capitalism did labor come to be described as having a price that would be set by the market. As we read Martin's descriptions of material objects, such as the funerary sacrifices of the Chinese "bourgeoisie" and the peasants (the differences between which she carefully delineates), we begin to see how the "factors of production"—particularly land and labor—resist their dissolution into precise money equivalents. Reading Martin's lectures it is borne in upon us that we need to understand that what things *are*, and what "commodity" *means*, are coefficients of the rules of the system within which they are being used.

In the third lecture, Martin turns to Malinowski in order to dramatize the way that labor and its end product become the basis of struggle. In a passage from *Coral Gardens and their Magic*, Malinowski describes how the Trobrianders dive for the flesh of the mollusk called *lapi*, meanwhile tossing to their children the handsome pearls inside the shells. These were worthless in the view of the Trobrianders, just as the flesh of the mollusc, being edible and judged delicious, possessed value. From the European perspective, of course, the Trobrianders had things exactly backward— they just did not know what things were worth. The economist, gazing in stunned silence, would soon declare triumphantly that the Trobrianders had a backward bending supply curve of labor. All they wanted from the traders was tobacco. When by their diving they had earned enough to pay for the tobacco they needed, they ceased to work. Faced by a Trobriand reality at the time, Europeans said "They don't get it—just when you raise their salaries, they decide to work less!" Thereupon two incongruent realities are refigured as a sort of battlefield, where the persons of the two economies then meet and jostle. The rules by which people live, by which they give order to their lives, thus become part of the struggle. In Emily Martin's work, the inclusion of the specific sites of such struggle lets us feel the dynamism inside all monetized economic systems.

I might remark upon one other aspect of Emily Martin's career and her Lectures. Emily was hired at Yale to strengthen the Department of Anthropology's offerings in the Asian field. But some of us there knew that she was not entirely happy with the way the definition of her skills might prove to be a constraint of a sort, ill fitting her rapidly growing interest in other sorts of anthropological study.

When Rich Price and I invited her to join us at Hopkins, she came down to visit and to meet some members of the Hopkins administration. Rich and I already knew what a good teacher she was. We found out, once she was here, how plucky she was, too. She was pregnant with her first child and had some tough morning sickness to struggle with daily, during that visit. But she completely won over the people at Hopkins.

Once she was here and teaching, she discovered for herself in what new and different directions she wanted to move intellectually. That meant forsaking to some extent her commitment to Asia. Even so, she continued to advise some of our best students in the Asia field, all the while building new fields of study, as her books would soon make plain. I count it an honor to have been able to watch her development over the years and perhaps in some small way to have been able to help.

EMILY MARTIN SPEAKS TO THE PRESENT, THIRTY YEARS ON

The relative absence of China as a key case in the development of analytics for a fully ethnographic, historical, and comparative anthropology of money has left a great gap in this field of study. China is, after all, one of the longest-running, and largest-administered, monetary economies in world history. A system of centralized currency issue goes back until at least the imperial period of the third century BC, and the linking of regional, and even microregional, economies through markets is very old. Twenty years before the composition of these lectures, G. William Skinner (1964) took a great step forward in the historical economic anthropology of China through his rich empirical and analytical study of markets and urban economies. Although he drew inspiration from European central place theory, Skinner's concept of articulated hierarchies of towns and markets, in roughly hexagonal shape, geographically juxtaposed to one another, drew on the work of Chinese scholars and brought a new socio-geographical concept into the existing "trade and markets" framework. The latter was based largely on a European model where "trade" was long-distance, often run by specialist merchants, and "markets" were provisioning systems shaped by the social and logistical situations of particular localities. China's specialization and trade circuits were different. Skinner argued strongly that theories of peasant economy needed to expand far beyond European feudal models, to include the highly productive small-scale production systems of Asia. He thought that the existing order of the Chinese countryside, as embodied in the marketplaces, actually constituted a kind of geographical resistance to imperial rule.

Emily Martin's lectures take this provocation into new fields that connect intimate life and cultural framings with larger structures and systemic dynamics. She was able to grasp enough historical and ethnographic sources to raise acute comparative and analytical questions for economic anthropology, without having to address the surge of changes that have emerged since 1989, attendant on globalization. There was enough historical material to make inferences. And the deeper cultural past could still be recaptured by fieldwork in rural Taiwan. By going as far as possible with these sources, she was able to raise fundamental questions of the kind that launched new thinking in anthropology: questions of the "dense meanings deposited in money" within intimate relations, while linking these to different dynamics of "accumulation," and, thereby, to a critical examination of our conceptual repertoire that comes largely from the moral, political, and conceptual economy of Europe, which was treated in our theoretical past as if it were a unique case of "the market economy."

Martin writes in configurational rather than typological terms: "elements of a capitalist economy can exist without implying that the whole system of capitalism as we know it is present." This takes any sense of inevitable logic or developmental progressivism out of the history of capitalism. Her position now converges with David Graeber's recent argument about China, namely that the Confucian state was "pro-market but anti-capitalist", and his quotation from Braudel that capitalism and markets could be conceived "as opposites" (Graeber 2011: 260). This is at the macro level. In local studies, her work resonates with new historical research as the remarkably detailed Chinese written record is increasingly recuperated for comparative scholarship.

The lectures go particularly deep into community norms and practices in order to show how the practices of money economies have worked within social life, both in China and the United States. Analytical questions arise. Particularly striking is the question of the relationship, in different monetary systems, among the classic functions of money: exchange, payment, unit-of-account, and store-of-value. In China, the store-of-value function of money was far less important than in Europe. Indeed the currency was explicitly dedicated to circulation. Deeply institutionalized markets did not produce capital accumulation. In China, the attendant "moral economy" (E. P. Thompson), "the social meaning of money" (Viviana Zelizer), and "the social life of money" (Nigel Dodd) nuance the relationship between money, sociality, and the occult within daily life quite differently from the Western tensions within capitalism—tensions that have otherwise been taken to be the prime framework for an integrated analysis of the economic system. Four topics seem particularly promising for engagement with current anthropological research: debt, markets, taxation, and moral economy (including kinship).

There is a surge of new interest in credit and debt within anthropology: in formal banking, in social life, and in the interstices of mutual accommodation and tension between the two (see, for example, the work of Deborah James [2014] in South Africa, and Gustav Peebles' [2010] more general overview of the mutuality of the two concepts in anthropology). For the study of community-level practices, Emily Martin introduces us here to sophisticated systems of debt calendrics, the irreducibility of certain elements of value—such as aspects of a bride's value—to monetary equivalence. Among her many detailed descriptions include: the complex around professional money-lenders and shop-keepers; modes of violent enforcement; recourse to the occult as a threatening presence to be mobilized by either side in the case of a failed repayment; the particular place of community associations; and the poetic metaphors for monetary life. Spirit money, occult retribution, apparently frequent suicide over unrepayable debt, disputes about the inheritance of debt, priority given to creating obligations rather than profits: these are all phenomena arising elsewhere, for which Martin's study can provide a valuable comparative touchstone. She points this out in several comparative passages in the lectures.

Martin's work can also now be linked to Akinobu Kuroda's (2012) fascinating historical comparison of the law and practice of debt and deferred payment accounting in China, Japan, and the United Kingdom. He concludes that where high quantities of small-denomination currency are supplied into a multiple currency system, as in China, deferred payment could be grounded in a highly developed unit-of-account system, which combined with cash circulation in commercial life. In single currency systems, with lower amounts of circulating media of exchange, regulated and legally-backed debt was more prevalent, as in Japan and the U.K. Like Martin, Kuroda (2012: 20) concludes that such differences among monetary systems "are diversified paths rather than evolutionary stages."

This moves us into markets and their organization. Following Skinner's seminal studies, Martin is able to connect market and culture in new ways. She departs from the classic concept of commodity, to write about everything that required money in order to be transacted, by referring to coin circulation practices from the third century, and by explaining the Chinese distinction between money in market sale and money in other transactions. Acquisition of people, labor, payment of wedding fees, taxes: all these mobilized money without passing through the market institutions to be considered as "commodities." So while "certain things could not be obtained without cash," the market-price nexus was not always in play.

The effects of taxation are alluded to through the policy motivations, but also through the monetary media through which people had to pay (silver) and therefore to the institutions for conversion of one currency to another. Similar issues arise in current concerns over the payment of taxes and fees, and people's accommodation of the calendrics of the formal sector. For the moment, this emerges mostly in the writings on debt, but doubtless there can be links made to the analysis of the lives of all money-relevant documents in economic life.

Finally, Martin's emphasis on the use of money to create and enact relationships, as distinct from the acquisition of things, gives us a bridge to explore systems that have been depicted as "wealth in people" (Guyer 1995), and investment in social relations (Berry 1980). The specific place of money in transactional repertoires, ongoing accounting, moral judgment, and strategic thinking within social life can be newly enriched by the detailed evidence supplied by the case Martin describes: where metal currency, state management of money supply, micro-regional specialization, and market commerce have a very long and well-documented history. Her study here is both an impetus to us to search for more sources from elsewhere, and an example for comparative and conceptual inspiration.

*

Although these lectures were first written almost thirty years ago, their concentrated theoretical, conceptual, and empirical content meets the growing work in the anthropology of money, not as a retrospective but as a stimulus for ongoing comparative and empirical ethnographic research into the actualities and possibilities for money and market systems. The places and eras, in both world history and intellectual history, where novel problematics have been engaged, continue to provide provocation for the kind of imaginative and rigorous new thinking for which anthropology as a discipline—and the ethnographic method as a philosophy of knowledge—continue to make their own contribution to the social science of the present. And, perhaps more importantly, they continue to depict realizable possibilities for the future. These lectures about the long-lasting and complex Chinese imperial monetary system, as distinct from the modern national monetary model, exemplify that contribution; they bring new history and new ethnography into sharp view, not only depicting but instigating new possibilities.

Jane I. Guyer and Sidney Mintz
Baltimore, February 2015

References

Ahern, Emily Martin. 1981. "The Thai Ti Kong Festival." In *The anthropology of Taiwanese society*, edited by Emily Martin Ahern and Hill Gates. Stanford: Stanford University Press.

———, and Hill Gates, eds. 1981. *The anthropology of Taiwanese society*. Stanford: Stanford University Press.

Anonymous. 1849. "The worship of ancestors among the Chinese." *The Chinese Repository* 18 (7): 363–84.

Balazs, Etienne. 1964. *Chinese civilization and bureaucracy*. Edited by Arthur F. Wright. Translated by H. M. Wright. New Haven and London: Yale University Press.

Ball, James Dyer. 1925. *Things Chinese or notes connected with China*. Shanghai, Hongkong, and Singapore: Kelley and Wash Ltd.

Baran, Paul A., and Paul M. Sweezy. 1966. *Monopoly capital: An essay on the American economic and social order*. New York: Monthly Review.

Bender, Thomas. 1978. *Community and social change in America*. Baltimore and London: Johns Hopkins University Press.

Berliner, Howard. 1982. "Medical modes of production." In *The problem of medical knowledge: Examining the social construction of medicine*, edited by Peter Wright and Andrew Press. Edinburgh: Edinburgh University Press.

Berry, Sara S. 1989. "Social institutions and access to resources: An introduction." *Africa* 59 (1): 1–5.

Blaxton, John. 1634. *The English usurer or, usury condemned.* Amsterdam and Norwood, NJ: Walter J. Johnson, Inc. and Theatrum Orb Terrarum.

Bohannan, Paul. 1967. "The impact of money on an African subsistance economy." In *Tribal and peasant economies,* edited by George Dalton. Austin and London: University of Texas Press.

Boone, Louis E., and David L. Kurtz, eds. 1976. *Contemporary business.* Hinsdale, IL: The Dryden Press.

Braverman, Harry. 1974. *Labor and monopoly capital: The degradation of work in the twentieth century.* New York: Monthly Review Press.

Brockman, John. 2004. "Gregory Bateson: The centennial." *Edge.* Conversations. November 9, 2004. http://edge.org/conversations/gregory-bateson-the-centennial.

Brown, Henry H. 1903. *Dollars want me: The new road to opulence.* London: Fowler and Company.

Butterworth, Eric. 1983. *Spiritual economics: The prosperity process.* Unity Village: Unity School.

Ch'u, Tsung-tsu. 1962. *Local government in China under the Ch'ing.* Stanford: Stanford University Press.

———. 1965. *Law and society in traditional China.* The Hague: Mouton and Company.

Clifford, James and George Marcus, eds. 1986. *Writing culture: The poetics and politics of ethnography.* Berkeley, CA: University of California Press.

Cohen, Abner. 1979. "Political symbolism." *Annual Review of Anthropology* 8 (1): 87–113.

Cohen, Myron L. 1976. *House united, house divided: The Chinese family in Taiwan.* New York and London: Columbia University Press.

Colletti, Lucio. 1975. "Introduction." In Karl Marx, *Early Writings.* Translated by Rodney Livingstone and Gregor Benton. Harmondsworth: Penguin.

Cornell, Richard D. 1985. "Evaluating a franchise opportunity." *Business,* December.

Crump, Thomas. 1981. *The phenomenon of money.* London and Boston: Routledge & Kegan Paul.

De Groot, J. J. M. 1967. *The religious system of China,* vol. 2, book 1. Taipei: Ch'eng-wen Publishing Company.

Diggins, John P. 1978. *The bard of savagery*. New York: The Seabury Press.

Dirlik, Arif. 1978. *Revolution and history*. Berkeley: University of California Press.

———. 1982. "Chinese historians and the Marxist concept of capitalism." *Modern China* 8 (1): 105–32.

Doolittle, Justus. 1865. *Social life of the Chinese, with some account of their religious, governmental, educational, and business customs and opinions with special but not exclusive reference to Fuhchau*, 2 vols. London: Samson Low, Son, and Marsten.

Dore, Henry. 1966. *Researches into Chinese superstitions*, vol. 1. Taipei: Ch'eng-Wen Publishing Company.

Dowie, Mark. 1979. "The corporate crime of the century." *Mother Jones*, November/December.

Edwards, Richard. 1979. *Contested terrain: The transformation of the workplace in the twentieth century*. New York: Basic Books.

Elvin, Mark. 1975. "Skills and resources in late traditional China." In *China's modern economy in historical perspective*, edited by Dwight H. Perkins. Stanford: Stanford University Press.

Engels, Friedrich. 1950. *The part played by labour in the transition from ape to man*. New York: International Publishers Co.

Engels, Friedrich and Eleanor B. Leacock. 1972. *The origin of the family, private property, and the state, in the light of the researches of Lewis H. Morgan*. New York: International Publishers Co.

Farnsworth, Clyde H. 1986. "China trade still growing." *The New York Times*, January 6: D2

Fei, Hsiao-tung. 1939. *Peasant life in China: A field study of country life in the Yangtse Valley*. London: Routledge.

———, and Chih-i chang. 1948. *Earthbound China*. London: Lund Humphries.

Feuchtwang, Stephan. 1974. "Domestic and communal worship in Taiwan." In *Religion and ritual in Chinese society*, edited by Arthur P. Wolf. Stanford: Stanford University Press.

Fielde, Adele. 1887. *Pagoda shadows: Studies from life in China*. Boston: Cortheel.

Fields, Rick, with Peggy Taylor, Rex Weyler, and Rick Ingrasci. 1984. *Chop wood, carry water: A guide to finding spiritual fulfillment in everyday life*. Los Angeles: J. P. Tarcher.

Fillmore, Charles. 1936. *Prosperity*. Unity Village: Unity Books.

Firth, Raymond. 1965. *Primitive Polynesian economy*. New York: W. W. Norton and Company, Inc.

Fisher, Marvin. 1966. "Melville's 'Bell-Tower': A double thrust."*American Quarterly* 8: 200–7.

———. 1967. *Workshops in the wilderness: The European response to American industrialization, 1830–1860*. Oxford: Oxford University Press.

Franke, Herbert. 1949. *Geld und Wirtschaft in China unter Mongolen-Herrschaft*. Leipzig: Otto Harrassowitz

Frece, John W. 1986. "Violations spread like virus, Prober says." *The Sun* (Baltimore), January 10: 1.

Freedman, Maurice. 1979a. "The handling of money: A note on the background to the economic sophistication of overseas Chinese." In *The study of Chinese society: Essays by Maurice Freedman*. Edited by G. William Skinner. Stanford: Stanford University Press.

———. 1979b. "Rites and duties, or Chinese marriage." In *The study of Chinese society: Essays by Maurice Freedman*. Edited by G. William Skinner. Stanford: Stanford University Press.

Freeman, James Dillet. 1978. *The story of Unity*. Unity Village: Unity Books.

Galambos, Louis. 1975. *The public image of big business in America, 1880–1940*. Baltimore and London: Johns Hopkins University Press.

Galbraith, John Kenneth. 1975. *Money: Whence it came, where it went*. Boston: Houghton Mifflin Company.

Ganog, William F. 1983. *Review of Medical Physiology*. Eleventh edition. Los Altos, CA: Lange.

Gates, Hill. 1987. "Money for the gods." *Modern China* 13 (3): 259–77.

Geertz, Clifford. 1962. "The rotating credit association: A middle 'rung' in development." *Economic Development and Cultural Change* 10 (3): 241–63.

Goodman, Ellen. 1983. "Life, if you've got the money." *The Commercial Appeal*, September 30: AS.

Graeber, David. 2011. *Debt. The first five thousand years*. Brooklyn, NY: Melville House Publishing

Gregory, C. A. 1980. "Gifts to men and gifts to God: Gift exchange and capital accumulation in contemporary Papua." *Man* 15 (4): 626–52.

————. 1982. *Gifts and commodities.* London: Academic Press.

Guyer, Jane I. 1995a. *Money matters: Instability, values, and social payments in the modern history of West African communities.* Portsmith, NH: Heinemann.

————. 1995b. "Wealth in people/wealth in things: An introduction." *Journal of African History* 36: 83–90.

————. 2004. *Marginal gains: Monetary transactions in Atlantic Africa.* Chicago: University of Chicago Press.

Guyton, Arthur C. 1984. *Physiology of the human body.* Sixth edition. Philadelphia: Saunders College Publishing.

————. 1986. *Textbook of medical physiology.* Seventh edition. Philadelphia: W. B. Saunders.

Habermas, Jürgen. 1973. "Was Heisst Heute Krise?" *Merkur* 4/5 (April/ May): 345–64.

Hareven, Tamara. 1982. *Family time and industrial time.* Cambridge: Cambridge University Press.

Harrell, C. Stevan. 1974. "When a ghost becomes a god." In *Religion and ritual in Chinese society*, edited by Arthur P. Wolf. Stanford: Stanford University Press.

————. 1981. "Effects of economic change in two Taiwanese villages." *Modern China* 7 (1): 31–54.

Harvey, David. 1982. *The limits to capital.* Chicago: University of Chicago Press.

————. 1985. "Time, space, money and the city." In *Consciousness and the urban experience.* Baltimore: Johns Hopkins University Press.

Henderson, Randi. 1983. "Demanding top dollar in the Cabbage Patch." *The Sun* (Baltimore), December 16: B1.

Hertz, Ellen. 1998. *The trading crowd: An ethnography of the Shanghai stock market.* Cambridge: Cambridge University Press.

Hertzberg, Daniel. 1986. "Poison pill defenses continue to grow as questions surround lockup options." *The Wall Street Journal*, January: 1.

Ho, Karen. 2009. *Liquidated: An ethnography of Wall Street.* Durham, NC: Duke University Press.

Ho, Ping-ti. 1964. *The ladder of success in Imperial China.* New York: John Wiley and Sons.

Hostetler, John A. 1980. *Amish society.* Baltimore: Johns Hopkins University Press.

Hou, Ching-lang. 1975. *Monnaies d'offrande et la notion de trésorerie dans la réligion chinoise*. Paris: Presses Universitaires de France.

Hsu, Robert C. 1985. "Conceptions of the market in post-Mao China." *Modern China* 11 (4): 436–60.

Huber, Richard M. 1971. *The American idea of success*. New York: McGraw-Hill Book Company.

Humphrey, Caroline. 1985. "Barter and economic disintegration." *Man* 20 (1): 48–72.

Hunter, Darn. 1937. *Chinese ceremonial paper*. Chillicothe, OH: The Mountain House Press.

Hurst, James Willard. 1956. *Law and the conditions of freedom*. Madison: University of Wisconsin Press.

———. 1982. *Law and markets in United States history*. Madison: University of Wisconsin Press.

Iowa Farm Unity Coalition. 1986. "Legislative positions and priorities of the Iowa Farm Unity Coalition." Ms.

James, Deborah. 2014. *Money from nothing. Indebtedness and aspiration in South Africa*. Palo Alto, CA: Stanford University Press.

Jennings, Humphrey. 1985. *Pandaemonium: 1660–1886*. New York: Free Press.

King, Frank H. H. 1965. *Money and monetary policy in China*. Cambridge, MA: Harvard University Press.

Kirkland, Edward Chase. 1956. *Dream and thought in the business community*. Ithaca: Cornell University Press,

Kuhn, Phillip H. 1984. "Chinese views of social classification." In *Class and social stratification in post-Revolution China*, edited by James L. Watson. Cambridge: Cambridge University Press.

Kulp, Daniel Harrison. 1925. *Country Life in South China*, vol. 1. Taipei: Ch'eng Wen Publishing Company (reprint 1966).

Kuroda, Akinobu. 2012. "Anonymous currencies or named debts? Comparison of currencies, local credits and units of account between China, Japan and England in the pre-industrial era." *Socio-Economic Review* 2012: 1–24

Leach, Edmund R. 1954. *Political systems of highland Burma*. Boston: Beacon Press.

Lee, Frederic E. 1926. *Currency, banking and finance in China*. Washington, DC: Government Printing Office.

Lewontin, R. C., Steven Rose, and Leon J. Kamin. 1984. *Not in our genes: Biology, ideology, and human nature.* New York: Pantheon.

Li Wei-tsu. 1948. "On the cult of the four sacred animals (四 大 門) in the neighborhood of Peking." *Folklore* 7 (1): 1–94.

Lipman, Joanne. 1986. "Vulture funds rise as property falls: Latest fad in real estate chills some experts." *The Wall Street Journal,* January 3: 4.

Little, Lester K. 1978. *Religious poverty and the profit economy in medieval Europe.* Ithaca: Cornell University Press.

Loewe, Michael. 1968. *Everyday life in early Imperial China.* New York: Harper & Row.

LoLordo, Ann. 1986. "S&L depositors brave cold to demand their money." *The Sun* (Baltimore), January 9: A1.

McAleavy, Henry. 1955. "Certain aspects of Chinese customary law in the light of Japanese scholarship." *London University's School of Oriental and African Studies Bulletin,* vol. 17. London: London University Press.

Macfarlane, Alan. 1985. "The root of all evil." In *The anthropology of evil,* ed. David Parkin. New York and Oxford: Basil Blackwell Ltd.

Malcolm, Andrew H. 1985a. "Troubled farmers: Debts and guns." *The New York Times,* December 12: A20.

———. 1985b. "Deaths on the Iowa Prairie: 4 new victims of economy." *The New York Times,* December 11: A1.

Malinowski, Bronisław. 1965. "Soil tilling and agricultural rites in the Trobriand Islands." In *Coral gardens and their magic,* vol. 1. Bloomington: Indiana University Press.

Marden, Orison Swett. 1917. *How to get what you want.* New York: Thomas Y. Crowell Company.

Marx, Karl. 1967. *Capital,* vol. I and vol. III. Edited by Friedrich Engels. New York: International Publishers Co.

———. 1973. *Grundrisse.* Edited by Martin Nicolaus. New York: Vintage Books.

———. 1975. *Early writings.* Introduced by Lucio Colletti. Translated by Rodney Livingstone and Gregor Benton. New York: Vintage Books.

———. 2006. *Capital: A critique of political economy.* Vol. 1. Translated by Ben Fowkes. New York: Penguin.

————, and Frederick Engels. 1970. *The German ideology*. Edited by C. J. Arthur. New York: International Publishers.

Mason, Elliott B. 1983. *Human physiology*. Menlo Park, CA: Benjamin/ Cummings Publishing Co.

Mauss, Marcel. 1967. *The gift*. New York: W. W. Norton and Company, Inc.

Maurer, Bill. 2011. *Mutual life, limited: Islamic banking, alternative currencies, lateral reason*. Princeton: Princeton University Press.

Mintz, Morton. 1985. *At any cost: Corporate greed, women, and the Dalkon Shield*. New York: Pantheon Books.

Mintz, Sidney W. 1964. "The employment of capital by market women in Haiti." In *Capital, saving and credit in peasant societies*, edited by Raymond Firth and B. S. Yamey. Chicago: Aldine Publishing Company.

————. 1974. *Worker in the cane: A Puerto Rican life history*. New York: W. W. Norton.

————. 1986. *Sweetness and power: The place of sugar in modern history*. New York: Penguin.

Moore, Barrington. 1972. *Reflections on the causes of human misery and upon certain proposals to eliminate them*. Boston: Beacon Press.

Moore, Robert Laurence. 1977. *In search of white crows: Spiritualism, parapsychology, and American culture*. Oxford: Oxford University Press.

Morgan, Lewis Henry. 1868. *The American beaver and his works*. Philadelphia: Lippincott.

————. 1877. *Ancient society*. New York: Henry Holt and Company.

————. 1881. *Houses and house-life of the American Aborigines*. Edited by Paul Bohannan. Chicago and London: University of Chicago Press (reprint 1965).

Morse, Hosea B. 1913. *The trade and administration of China*. New York: Longmans, Green and Company.

Mumford, Lewis. 1967. *The myth of the machine: Technics and human development*. New York: Harcourt, Brace and World.

Myer, Donald. 1965. *The positive thinkers*. New York: Doubleday.

Nader, Laura. 1969. "Up the anthropologist—Perspectives studying up." In *Reinventing anthropology*, edited by Dell Hymes. New York: Random House.

Neale, Walter C. 1976. *Monies in society*. San Francisco: Chandler and Sharp Publishers, Inc.

Needham, Joseph. 1956. *Science and civilization in China*, 7 vols. Cambridge: Cambridge University Press.

Nelson, Benjamin N. 1949. *The idea of usury*. Princeton: Princeton University Press.

Newman, Eric P. 1967. *The early paper money of America*. Racine, WI: Whitman

Noonan, John T. 1957. *The scholastic analysis of usury*. Cambridge, MA: Harvard University Press.

Nordlinger, Stephen E. 1985. "Farmers' crisis produces a crop of bank failures." *The Sun* (Baltimore), March 10: A1

Olesker, Michael. 1986. "Levitts appear passively disdainful at court hearing." *The Sun* (Baltimore), January 9: A1.

Ostling, Richard N. 1986. "Power, glory and politics." *Time*, February 17: 62–69.

Parry, Johnathan P. 1985. "The gift, the Indian gift, and the 'Indian gifter'." *Ms.*

Peebles, Gustav. 2010. "The anthropology of credit and debt." *Annual Review of Anthropology* 39: 224–40.

Perkins, Dwight H. 1969. *Agricultural development in China 1368–1968*. Chicago: Aldine Publishing Company.

Philips, Michael. 1974. *The seven laws of money*. Menlo Park, CA, and New York: World Wheel and Random House.

Poe, Edgar Allen. 1889. *The gold bug*. New York: Putnam's.

Polanyi, Karl. 1944. *The great transformation*. Boston: Beacon Press.

Ponder, Catherine. 1962. *The dynamic laws of prosperity: Forces that bring riches to you*. Englewood Cliffs, NJ: Prentice-Hall.

———. 1964. *The prosperity secret of the ages: How to channel a golden river of riches into your life*. Englewood Cliffs, NJ: Prentice-Hall.

———. 1966. *The dynamic laws of healing*. Camarillo, CA: Devorss & Company.

———. 1968. *Pray and grow rich*. West Nyack, NY: Parker Publishing Co.

———.1971. *Open your mind to prosperity*. Unity Village: Unity Books.

———. 1976. *The millionaires of Genesis*. Marina del Rey, CA: DeVorss.

———. 1977. *The millionaire Moses*. Marina del Rey, CA: DeVorss.

———. 1978. *The millionaire Joshua*. Marina del Rey, CA: DeVorss.

————. 1979. *The millionaire from Nazareth*. Marina del Rey, CA: DeVorss.

Price, Richard. 2002. *First-time: The historical vision of an African American people*. Chicago: University of Chicago Press.

Rawski, Evelyn Sakakida. 1972. *Agricultural change and the peasant economy of South China*. Cambridge, MA: Harvard University Press.

Report of the special counsel on the savings and loan crisis. 1986. Baltimore.

Resek, Carl. 1960. *Lewis Henry Morgan: American scholar*. Chicago and London: University of Chicago Press.

Rehert, Isaac. 1986. "Down on the farm." *The Sun* (Baltimore), February: D1.

Rivière, Peter. 1985. "The Warnock Report." *Anthropology Today* 1 (4): 2–7.

Robbins, William. 1986. "Farm belt suicides reflect greater hardship and deepening despondency." *The New York Times*, January 14: A11.

Rodgers, Daniel T. 1974. *The work ethic in industrial America*. Chicago and London: University of Chicago Press.

Russell, Robert A. 1950. *You, too, can be prosperous*. Marina del Rey, CA: DeVorss.

Salisbury, Harrison E. 1989. *A time of change: A reporter's tale of our time*. Toronto: HarperCollins Canada, Ltd.

Salisbury, Richard F. 1973. "Economic anthropology." *Annual Review of Anthropology* 2 (1): 85–94.

Samuelsson, Kurt. 1973. "Religion and economic action." In *Protestantism, capitalism, and social science*, edited by Robert W. Green. Lexington, Toronto, and London: D. C. Heath and Company.

Schabacker, Joseph C. 1971. *Strengthening small business management*. Washington, D.C.: Small Business Administration.

Seaman, Gary. 1982. "Spirit money: An interpretation." *Journal of Chinese Religions* 10: 80–91.

Sedgewick, Eve K. 1985. *Between men: English literature and male homosexual desire*. New York: Columbia University Press.

Schneider, Harold K. 1975. "Economic development and anthropology." *Annual Review of Anthropology* 4: 271–92.

Schoenberger, Erica. 2014. *Nature, choice and social power*. New York: Routledge.

Shiga, Shuzo. 1978. "Family property and the law of inheritance in historical China." In *Chinese family law and social change in historical and comparative perspective*, edited by David C. Buxbaum. Seattle and London: University of Washington Press.

Silin, Robert H. 1976. *Leadership and values: The organization of large-scale Taiwanese enterprises.* Cambridge, MA, and London: Harvard University Press.

Simmel, Georg. 1950. "The metropolis and mental life." In *The sociology of Georg Simmel.* Edited by Kurt H. Wolff. New York: Free Press.

———. 1978. *The philosophy of money.* Translated by Tom Bottomore and David Frisby. Boston, London, and Melbourne: Routledge & Kegan Paul.

Skinner, G. William. 1964. "Marketing and social structure in Rural China, part I." *The Journal of Asian Studies* 24 (1): 1–43.

Smith, Arthur H. 1970. *Village life in China.* Boston: Little, Brown, and Company.

Smith, Carol A. 1974. "Economics of marketing systems: Models from economic geography." *Annual Review of Anthropology* 3 (1): 167–201.

Sohn-Rethel, Alfred. 1983. *Intellectual and manual labor.* Translated by Martin Sohn-Rethel. Atlantic Highlands, NJ: Humanities Press.

Sontag, Susan. 1979. *Illness as metaphor.* New York: Vintage.

Stacey, Judith. 1983. *Patriarchy and socialist revolution in China.* Berkley: University of California Press.

Stack, Carol. 1974. *All our kin: Strategies for survival in a black community.* New York: Harper & Row.

Stites, David. 1982. "Small-scale industry in Yingge, Taiwan." *Modern China* 8 (2): 247–79.

Su, Jing, and Luo Lun. 1978. *Landlord and labor in late Imperial China: Case studies from Shandong.* Cambridge, MA, and London: Harvard University Press.

Sullam, Brian. 1986. "S&L 'insider deals' found commonplace." *The Sun* (Baltimore), January 12: A1.

Sung, Lung-sheng. 1981. "Property and family division." In *The anthropology of Taiwanese society*, edited by Emily Martin Ahern and Hill Gates. Stanford: Stanford University Press.

Tawney, Richard H. 1929. *Religion and the rise of capitalism.* London: John Murray.

————. 1966. *Land and labor in China*. Boston: Beacon Press.

Tett, Gillian. 2009. *Fool's gold: The inside story of J. P. Morgan and how Wall Street greedc corrupted its bold dream and created a financial catastrophe*. New York: Free Press.

Therborn, Göran. 1980. *The ideology of power and the power of ideology*. London: Verso.

Thompson, E. P. 1967. "Time, work-discipline, and industrial capitalism." *Past and Present* 38: 56–97.

Troeltsch, Ernst. 1956. *The social teachings of the Christian churches*, vol. 2. Translated by olive Wyon. London: George Allen and Unwin Ltd.; New York: The Macmillan Company.

Turner, Victor W. 1975. "Symbolic Studies." *Annual Review of Anthropology*. 4 (1): 145–61.

Twitchett, Denis. 1968. "Merchant, trade, and government in late T'ang." *Asia Major* 14: 63–95.

Vander, Arthur J., James H. Sherman, and Dorothy S. Luciano. 1980. *Human physiology: The mechanisms of body function*. Third edition. New York: McGraw Hill.

Walzer, Michael. 1983. *Spheres of justice: A defense of pluralism and justice*. New York: Basic Books.

Watson, James L., ed. 1980 *Asian and African systems of slavery*. Oxford: Basil Blackwell; Berkeley: University of California Press.

Watson, Rubie S. 1985. *Inequality among brothers: Class and kinship in South China*. Cambridge and New York: Cambridge University Press.

Weber, Max. 1958. *The protestant ethic and the spirit of capitalism*. Translated by Talcott Parsons. New York: Scribner.

Wells, David A. 1896. *Robinson Crusoe's money*. New York: Greenwood Press (1969 reprint).

White, Leslie A., ed. 1959. *Lewis Henry Morgan: The Indian Journals 1859–62*. Ann Arbor: University of Michigan Press.

Williams, Raymond. 1980. *Problems in materialism and culture*. London: Verso

————. 1981. *The sociology of culture*. New York: Schocken Books.

Winner, Langdon. 1977. *Autonomous technology: Technics-out-of-control as a theme in political thought*. Cambridge, MA: MIT Press.

Wolf, Eric R. 1981. "The mills of inequality: A Marxian approach." In *Social inequality: Comparative and developmental approaches*, edited by Gerald D. Berreman. London: Academic Press.

Wolf, Margery. 1985. *Revolution postponed: Women in contemporary China.* Stanford: Stanford University Press.

Woolf, Virginia 1929. *A room of one's own.* New York and London: Harcourt Brace Jovanovich.

Worrall, Ambrose, and Olga Worrall. 1965. *The gift of healing.* New York: Harper & Row.

Wright, J. Patrick. 1979. *On a clear day you can see General Motors.* New York: Avon Books.

Wu, David Y. H. 1974. "To kill three birds with one stone: The rotating credit associations of the Papua New Guinea Chinese." *American Ethnologist* 1 (3): 565–84.

Wu, Leonard T. K. 1936. "Merchant capital and usury capital in rural China." *Far Eastern Survey* 5 (7): 63–68.

Yang, Liansheng. 1952. *Money and credit in China: A short history.* Cambridge, MA: Harvard University Press.

Young, John Aubrey. 1974. *Business and sentiment in a Chinese market town.(Asian folklore and social life monographs.).* Taipei: The Orient Cultural Service.

Zinn, Howard. 1980. *A people's history of the United States.* New York: Harper & Row.

Index

Hau Books is committed to publishing the most distinguished texts in classic and advanced anthropological theory. The titles aim to situate ethnography as the prime heuristic of anthropology, and return it to the forefront of conceptual developments in the discipline. *Hau* Books is sponsored by some of the world's most distinguished anthropology departments and research institutions, and releases its titles in both print editions and open-access formats.

www.haubooks.com

Supported by

Hau-N. E. T.

Network of Ethnographic Theory

University of Aarhus – EPICENTER (DK)
University of Amsterdam (NL)
University of Bergen (NO)
Brown University (US)
California Institute of Integral Studies (US)
University of Canterbury (NZ)
University of Chicago (US)
University of Colorado Boulder Libraries (US)
CNRS – Centre d'Études Himalayennes (FR)
Cornell University (US)
University of Edinburgh (UK)
The Graduate Institute, Geneva Library (CH)
University of Helsinki (FL)
Johns Hopkins University (US)
University of Kent (UK)
Lafayette College Library (US)
Institute of Social Sciences of the University of Lisbon (PL)
University of Manchester (UK)
The University of Manchester Library (UK)
Max-Planck Institute for the Study of Religious and Ethnic Diversity
at Göttingen, (Library) (DE)
Museu Nacional – UFRJ (BR)
Norwegian Museum of Cultural History (NO)
University of Oslo (NO)
University of Oslo Library (NO)
Pontificia Universidad Católica de Chile (CL)
Princeton University (US)
University of Queensland (AU)
University of Rochester (US)
Universidad Autónoma de San Luis Potosi (MX)
University of Sydney (AU)

www.haujournal.org/haunet